ACADEMIA LUNARE
Call For Papers 2016

Gender Identity and Sexuality in Current Fantasy and Science Fiction

Edited By
Francesca T Barbini

Editor Introduction © Francesca T Barbini 2017
Articles © is with each individual author 2017
Cover Design © Francesca T Barbini 2017
(based on 'Portrait of a Lady' by R van der Weyden)

First published by Luna Press Publishing 2017

Gender Identity and Sexuality in Current Fantasy and Science Fiction © 2017. All rights reserved. No part of this publication may be reproduced, stored in a retrieval system, or transmitted in any form or by any means, electronic, mechanical, photocopy, recording or otherwise, without prior written permission of the copyright owners. Nor can it be circulated in any form of binding or cover other than that in which it is published and without similar condition including this condition being imposed on a subsequent purchaser.

www.lunapresspublishing.com

ISBN-13: 978-1-911143-24-6

Contents

Introduction   v

The Myth of Meritocracy and the Reality of the Leaky Pipe and Other Obstacles in Science Fiction & Fantasy
By Juliet E McKenna   1

Bikini Armour: women characters, readers and writers in male narratives
By Anna Milon   37

Gender-identity and sexuality in current sub-genres of British fantasy literature: do we have a problem?
By A J Dalton   57

Tipping the Fantastic: How the Transgender Tipping Point Has Influenced Speculative Fiction
By Cheryl Morgan   83

Badass Bisexual Babes: Shameless Titillation or Empowered Characters Embracing Their True Selves and Sexuality?
By Hazel Butler   105

Doll Parts: Reflections of the Feminine Grotesque in Frances Hardinge's Cuckoo Song and Neil Gaiman's Coraline
By Kim Lakin-Smith   131

Subversion, Sex, and Violence: Rape as Narrative Tool in 'A Song of Ice and Fire'
By Lorianne Reuser   155

The Magical Way Forward? - Recent Changes in Gender Representation in 'Magic: The Gathering' Card Game
By Rostislav Kůrka   181

What about Tauriel? From Divine Mothers to Active Heroines - The female roles in J. R. R. Tolkien's Legendarium and Peter Jackson's movie adaptations
By Jyrki Korpua   207

Newly Added Female Characters to Blockbuster Franchises: Gender Balancing in Otherwise Male-Dominated Fictional Worlds or a Greater Purpose?
By Alina Hadîmbu   229

Biographies   239

Introduction

In 2016, Luna Press opened its very first Call for Papers. Under the umbrella title of "Gender identity and sexuality in Current Fantasy and Science Fiction: do we have a problem?", we invited writers to explore the theme from their own personal perspectives and inclinations.

The result was as incredible as it was diverse. The papers you are about to read explore how society, as reflected in real life, literature, movies, TV, games and cosplay, is currently dealing with gender identity and sexuality in speculative fiction.

At Luna, we believe that the critical assessment of speculative fiction can only be of benefit, as it functions as a mirror for society. Moreover, it allows readers to delve deeper into the work of a creator, generating more scope for appreciation or constructive criticism.

I do hope you enjoy this collection.

Francesca T Barbini
Editor

The Myth of Meritocracy and the Reality of the Leaky Pipe and Other Obstacles in Science Fiction & Fantasy

By Juliet E McKenna

It was initially assumed that increased female entry into careers such as law, medicine and higher education would naturally result in more equal representation at the higher levels over time. This has been proven not to be the case. This paper will consider what evidence from such research is equally applicable to lack of diversity in genre publishing, and what factors might be specific to SF&F.

It was initially assumed that increased female entry into careers such as law, medicine and higher education would naturally result in more equal representation at the higher levels over time. This has been proven not to be the case. We now see women writers and those from other under-represented racial and LGBT populations entering the SF & Fantasy genres in increasing numbers. Indeed, women have been writing in these genres since they first appeared. However, lists of bestsellers and of authors with long-term and sustained writing careers are still dominated by men. Let us consider what evidence from relevant research in other disciplines might apply to the issue of diversity in genre publishing, and see what factors might be specific to SF & Fantasy.

Studies of gender and other representation in the workplace have generated a specific jargon among human resources managers and other interested groups. For those in the SF&F world, these terms can seem equally applicable to a fantasy adventure quest.

The Gatekeeper

The first challenge is getting past the Gatekeepers. Are women and people of colour being deliberately excluded? The demonstrable persistence of such overt discrimination in the industry has demanded legislation to counter it, after all.

When looking for evidence of Gatekeepers in SF&F, it is immediately apparent that women are now well represented at the highest levels of genre publishing, as commissioning editors and editorial directors in both the UK and the US. This is not to say women cannot be misogynist or subject to other prejudices but the numbers of new books from different groups being promoted for 2017 would argue against gross, systemic bias at this entry stage. Barnes & Noble's list of 96 titles recommended by SF and Fantasy editors (Cunningham, 2017) has 48 titles by authors readily identifiable as men, compared to the rest. The Verge website's article (Liptak, 2017) on 33 SF and fantasy titles 'that everyone will be talking about in 2017' offers 18 titles by self-evidently male authors.

There is certainly no evidence that women are somehow inferior writers, compared to men. In recent years, female authors have been well-represented in both nominations and wins for all the major SF & Fantasy prizes. Between 2011 and 2015, four women won the Arthur C Clarke Award (ACCA, 2016) Women dominated the 2013 Nebula Awards

(SFWA, 2013).

There is similarly no evidence that readers will naturally or inevitably discriminate on the grounds of gender. Short story competitions where judges see submissions stripped of author names and other identifying data consistently produce gender balanced shortlists. This has been my own experience as a judge for a Book Club Associates competition, the James White Short Story Award and the Deddington Literary Festival. Even where authors can be identified, provided readers focus on the content above all else, gender balance follows. Epic fantasy author and best-seller Mark Lawrence has run 'The Self-Published Fantasy Blog Off' for the past two years, in which ten review websites assess the books submitted. In 2016, the 10 finalists were 5 male and 5 female authors, from an overall field of 300 books, of which 49% were submitted by men (Lawrence, 2016).

However this does not mean that participation is consistently equal. The Strange Horizons website's SF Count (Cosh, 2016) has measured participation by looking at the gender balance of male versus female authors as recorded by Locus magazine's 'Books Received' listings. In their 2015 report, looking at author gender in 2014, "this year's proportion of books by women/non-binary individuals is the lowest recorded in the SF Count to date, both overall (39.9%) and in the US (42.0%) and UK (31.3%)." So are there Gatekeepers at work?

Genre editors, male and female alike, insist they would publish more women if they had more submissions from them. This mirrors findings in academic publishing when under-representation of women in journals has been examined (West, Jacquet, King, Correll and Bergstrom, 2013). Research across a range of disciplines has found that women consistently hold themselves and their work to a higher standard than male colleagues, with the result that they are far more reluctant to put their work forward for publication (Correll, 2004). Since this persistent problem is rooted in cultural issues, there is no reason to suppose that SF&F writers are somehow immune. Indeed, creative writing tutors consistently report an excess of confidence among male students compared to an excess of diffidence among women writers at the pre-publication stage.

Successive studies have also shown that academic papers of equal quality are more likely to be accepted from male authors than from women. We certainly need to consider this possibility in relation to fiction and when considering the role of literary agents. In 2015 Catherine Nichols began sending out the same novel to agents, male and female, under a male pseudonym as well as in her own name (Nichols, 2015). "Total data: George sent out 50 queries, and had his manuscript requested 17 times. He is eight and a half times better than me at writing the same book. Fully a third of the agents who saw his query wanted to see more, where my numbers never did shift from one in 25."

Is this indicative of overt discrimination or a more subtle problem? Where under-representation in other fields has been examined, the Halo Effect has become apparent. In personnel management, this signifies the unconscious inclination of recruiters to favour those candidates who are most like them. This has long been identified as a key cause of 'male and pale' predominance in the upper echelons of the civil service, the judiciary, Parliament and the City of

London, to name but a few. Conversely, the Horns Effect hampers candidates with significantly different backgrounds to key decision makers, where unconsciously negative assumptions are made.

How could this be relevant to SF & Fantasy? Well, the Horns Effect can certainly be seen at work in Hollywood, where 'everybody knows' that female-led superhero movies lack box-office appeal. The commercial and critical failure of films like *Catwoman* (2004) and *Elektra* (2005) is cited as indisputable evidence, solely on the basis of having a female lead, whenever any Wonder Woman movie is mooted (we can only hope that the recent successes of Rogue One, The Force Awakens and the all-female Ghostbusters will change this perception). Conversely, the lacklustre performance of *Daredevil* (2003) or *Green Lantern* (2011) apparently has no bearing on the ongoing multi-film projects from Marvel and DC. A broad range of explanations has been found for those particular films underperforming which have little or nothing to do with the lead star's gender.

In terms of books, we should consider the predominance of male authors on bestseller lists and remember that publishing is first and foremost the business of selling books in an increasingly challenging retail climate. Authors consistently report rejections from agents, male and female, citing their book as lacking 'breakout' potential. The possibility of unconscious bias must be acknowledged, if 'everybody knows' SF & Fantasy written by men is more likely to sell – because that's what everybody sees selling best. This particular Halo Effect may well influence publishing decisions, especially now that marketing departments have at least as much say as editorial in some publishing companies. Anecdotal evidence certainly suggests that female authors are encouraged by agents and editors alike, to consider writing Young Adult fiction far more frequently than their male colleagues, on the basis of established female bestsellers in that field.

This predominance of male writers in mass-market SF & Fantasy can have a further, subtle influence on gender representation. Role models matter, at the entry level and throughout women's careers in every area where gender imbalance has been studied. Their presence is key to encouraging and increasing participation. When considering the likelihood of unconscious bias in SF & Fantasy publishing both in terms of women limiting themselves, we should return to the gender balance statistics cited so far.

The Barnes & Noble's list of 96 titles cited earlier has 48 titles by authors readily identifiable as men but 31 by self-evidently female authors alongside 10 where gender is obscured by unfamiliar or gender neutral names, or initials. The Verge article offers 18 titles by identifiably male authors alongside 14 by women and 4 gender-neutral writers. The Self-Published Fantasy Blog Off 2016 received 300 books, of which 49% were submitted by visibly male writers, 33% by female writers and 18% gender neutral. In 2016, the 10 finalists were 4 self-evidently male and 2 self-evidently female authors, alongside 4 gender neutral through the use of initials.

So while male participation is apparent at around the 50% mark, visible female participation drops to between 30 – 40 %. Even if this gender-neutral category was actually all women writers that still means hopeful writers have fewer obviously female role models. In fact, closer examination, particularly of unfamiliar names, demonstrates that this gender neutral category invariably includes men. So male participation is in fact higher than that gender-balanced 50% or so seen at first glance.

'Best of' lists and articles surveying the history of Science Fiction and Fantasy persistently focus on male writers, excluding women's contribution to the development of the genre. Where women are cited, we frequently see the same, very few, names repeated, and discussion of books often published decades ago, giving the impression that women are not currently active in a particular area. This arguably contributes to instances of agents and editors unconsciously ascribing as yet unproven potential to male authors.

Examples from magazines and the Internet are too numerous to cite. This problem was epitomised by the BBC's recent documentary series 'Paperback Heroes' (Marr, 2016) which broadcast a programme on Epic Fantasy on 24th October 2016. The programme featured discussion of the work of seven major writers who were six men and one, perhaps two, women if we include the very passing reference to J K Rowling. The woman whose work was discussed in some depth? Ursula Le Guin, and the book was A Wizard of Earthsea, first published in 1968.

Four male writers were interviewed and one woman who was interviewed solely in the context of fantasy for children. Of all the writers included, adding in cover shots or single-sentence name checks, eleven men featured, compared to six women. Of those women, three got no more than a name check and one got no more than a screenshot of a single book.

All these featured and interviewed writers are deservedly

popular, irrespective of genre, their books widely read, and their work is illustrative of points well worth making about fantasy. But those same points could have been made just as effectively while featuring a more gender-balanced selection of writers, from the genre's origins to the present day. Doing so would have offered new writers a far more representative range of role models, encouraging them to try their chances with an agent or an editor.

The Sticky Floor

This lack of visibility for women and writers of colour contributes significantly to the next challenge facing those authors who've managed to get past the Gatekeepers. The Sticky Floor is a widely used term for the failure of women to progress upwards through an organisation or a profession at the same rate as men, even when entry is 50/50 by gender.

Let us consider the longer term effects of that BBC programme on Epic Fantasy. This skewed gender selection of featured authors guarantees that these are the books getting a sales boost from such high-level exposure. When the next programme maker comes along to see what's popular, maybe with a view to a dramatisation or to feature in a documentary, he'll see that same male-dominated landscape. So that will influence the selection of books getting the next chance of appearing on screen. Thus the self-fulfilling prophecy of promoting what sells, thereby guaranteeing that's what sells best, continues to entrench gender bias.

Bookshops show the same tendency towards gender-skewed promotion, particularly in SF & Fantasy. The annual reappearance of Game of Thrones in TV listings invariably prompts bookshop displays offering readers a range of epic fantasy titles on the basis of 'If you like George RR Martin, try this!'. These selections are invariably male-dominated and frequently entirely male-authored, thus erasing the many women writers currently working in this particular sub-genre.

In 2014 I enlisted the help of readers and fans online to gather some firm data on this issue. Volunteers recorded the gender balance of the books on special offer and promotional tables in the UK's last remaining national bookshop chain, Waterstones (McKenna, 2014). Twenty shops were surveyed out of 275 branches, from May to July.

On the general Buy One Get One Half Price tables, in all but one instance the gender balance ranged from 45% male/55% female to 65% male/35% female and was evenly spread across that range, so for all intents and purposes, we can consider that a 50/50 split. The 50/50 split was even clearer in the Summer Reading promotional tables. Though individual tables might be seriously skewed in larger branches, with one offering chick-lit and romance by exclusively female authors alongside another offering thrillers all by men. But that's at least as much a reflection of what's written and published as it is of marketing choices.

However different pictures emerged when looking at books by genre. Any preconception that Children's and Young Adult writing is dominated by women didn't hold up when it came to promotion. The gender spread was pretty equal over all though there were more individual instances of markedly skewed displays. One bookshop had a table with 85% male authors while another had one with 60%

women writers. Crime showed an even greater range of variation. There were as many tables with more than 50% female authors as there were with more than 50% men overall but these varied from 100% male (Euro Crime) to one with below 40% male authors.

In SF & Fantasy? There were no tables with less than 55% male authors with the single exception of one SF&F Buy One Get One Half Price table in a large, city centre branch with an established reputation for its excellent genre range. Of the 21 SF&F promotional tables counted, 17 were 75% male authors or more. 5 were 95-100% male, including one all-male offering Future Noir SF. Where stores are large enough to separate out SF from Fantasy, the bias against women in SF was even more marked than that in fantasy. In most shops, Horror is folded into SF&F but in three instances where Horror got its own table (not included in that total of 21), those were all 95% male authors.

There were three instances, not included in the overall count of tables, of all-female SF&F tables in large, city centre branches. This is a mixed blessing. While it's welcome visibility, it also makes women writers much easier to ignore and risks perpetuating the notion that female authors are somehow different and not integrated into the mainstream of the genre.

There's also more to this than simply the numbers. As one respondent said, 'I don't actually bother looking at the SF&F table these days. It'll just be this year's books by men I don't read anyway.' The same names recur time and again. This does as much disservice to those other male authors who rarely, if ever, benefit from this level of promotion as it does to the women writers who are so routinely ignored. All of which is commercially short-sighted.

The same gender bias is apparent in promotional material emailed to readers by online booksellers. I analysed 23 of Waterstones' monthly promotional emails sent to loyalty card holders, from March 2012 to June 2014. Book of the Month choices were equally shared between male and female authors, with the proviso that women are over-represented in children's and romance choices, and men dominate other areas. Every single non-fiction History choice was by a man. Moving on, 75% of the New Book titles appearing at the top of these emails were written by men. Of the Backlist promotions, 70% were for male authors. Promotional banner adverts at the top of each email offered books 60% of which were written by men. Similar skew was apparent in the 'Coming Soon' selection, appearing below New Books and offering 65% male-authored titles. The Books in the Media selection featured 76% male writers and Reviewed in the Newspapers offered 70% male-authored titles.

Review coverage shows a similar bias. VIDA, the Women in Literary Arts organisation, began monitoring gender representation in American literary magazines and journals in 2009 (VIDA, 2012). Year on year, they have found that the majority of books enjoying such publicity are written by men, and are reviewed by men. Women reviewers are far more likely to review books across the gender spectrum. In recent years, VIDA have also expanded their survey to take into account race and ethnicity, gender, sexual identity, and ability, finding a similar lack of proportionate representation.

The Strange Horizons website was inspired to begin their own survey of review coverage for SF & Fantasy titles in 2010 (Cosh, 2016b). Their most recent survey finds

60% of titles reviewed by genre magazines and websites were written by male authors. Reviewers are predominately male (56%) and overwhelmingly white (90%). High profile magazines are frequently towards the more biased end of the scale. Looking at SFX magazine's 2015 coverage only 29% of their reviews featured books by women and non-binary authors. Locus magazine's 50% rating was only achieved thanks to Carolyn Cushman's column offering 8-10 capsule reviews per issue, of which 80% are of books by women. Since this survey began, many magazines and websites have improved their coverage but there is still a long way to go before representation is anywhere near proportionate.

This lack of visibility significantly hampers women authors who are trying to get free of the Sticky Floor. It remains true that word of mouth sells books, irrespective of gender. To return to those Waterstones promotional emails, the 'Books You Love' driven by actual sales offered a selection of titles 48% of which were written by men, 46% by women and 6% which were gender neutral by virtue of initials or an unusual name. In 'Staff Picks' and 'What We're Reading' selections, choices are 53% male, 47% female. But these sections were always right at the bottom of the email, thus far less prominent and far more likely to be overlooked by someone scanning an email in a hurry. If people are going to talk about a book, they have to know it exists.

It is said that 48% of Amazon purchases are generated by targeted searches rather than idle browsing. People go looking for what they want to buy. How are they going to go looking online for books by women which they don't even know exist? When considering the impact of this disparity in visibility, it is instructive to look at the David Gemmell Awards for Fantasy, compared to a juried prize like the Arthur C Clarke Award. The Gemmells are a popular vote, and the organisers put a great deal of effort into getting publishers to nominate, and readers to consider books by women authors and writers of colour. The results are however persistently male-dominated, with voters gravitating to those books and authors which get the lion's share of the publicity available for the epic fantasy genre.

These books are deservedly popular, written by hardworking authors and produced to a high standard by professional editorial teams, with sales driven by eager fans recommending them to other keen readers. If this wasn't the case, these books would not sell. There are plenty of instances in book-selling history to prove that hype alone cannot shift books; the novel 'Swan' published under model Naomi Campbell's name is the archetypal example within the trade. But the fact remains that if books by women and writers of colour do not get an equal share of publicity and promotional opportunities, readers do not have the same opportunities to notice their books, to buy them, to read and recommend them. These authors will not sell in the same quantities, and their progress up the ranks of writers is accordingly slower.

Retail is a numbers-driven business, whatever is being sold. When a book-selling chain's marketing department looks at male-dominated sales figures to pick popular authors as safe bets for front-of-store promotion, they will apparently see proof of the insidious myth that SF&F by women doesn't sell. If it won't sell, there's no profit in promoting it. So books written by women aren't among those offered for sale, often at insidiously attractive discounts, which further boost male-dominated sales. Thus the self-fulfilling prophecy is reinforced.

Other factors have been identified in different professions and industries which contribute to women finding themselves on a Sticky Floor. Decades ago, women's failure to progress through organisations was attributed to lack of commitment. When it was pointed out that the main measure of this lack of commitment was women's failure to progress, thus making this a completely circular argument, other measures of commitment were sought. One that has proved robust across various disciplines is 'organisational citizenship', which is to say participation in activities such as workplace union and employee welfare programmes, outreach to the wider community and mentoring within the organisation, particularly when it comes to supporting newcomers from under-represented groups.

Once again, it is illuminating to see which of those apply in SF & Fantasy. Historically it was claimed that women's participation as writers was limited because women as readers and writers alike were simply not particularly interested in the genre. Looking for measures of 'organisational citizenship', it is immediately clear that this is nonsense. Women play a significant and active role in organisations such as SFWA, a professional writers' organisation, and fan organisations such as the BSFA and the BFS. Women authors have been the driving force behind collective initiatives such as Broad Universe and Book View Cafe. Women are also well represented in con-running circles, one of the invaluable elements of the SF & Fantasy genre offering visibility and publicity opportunities for writers. Attendance at conventions by readers and writers alike is now no longer male dominated, though people of colour and other minorities remain under-represented. There is no justification for claiming any lack of commitment by women writers or fans.

However, in common with other industries and professions, it can be seen that such organisational citizenship in SF & Fantasy comes at a measurable cost to women. Men are much better at safeguarding time to be used to their own direct advantage, while women remain culturally conditioned to help out and to feel bad about saying 'No'. But time spent on activities which benefit the group or the genre as a whole cannot be spent on activities which directly benefit an individual's career.

For example, participating in anthologies offers all authors a valuable opportunity to put their work in front of potential new readers. However, editors consistently report under-submission from women, as well as far higher success rate among those women who do offer work, indicating that the same issues of confidence already explored apply here. There is also evidence that women authors can simply find themselves too busy to take advantage of such invitations. Ian Whates of Newcon Press, and Mark Morris when editing a book on the work of British scriptwriter Nigel Kneale, have both been challenged over gender imbalances in different projects' contributors. This is hardly a surprise, given how common male-only and male-dominated anthologies still are, thanks to male editors lazily selecting only the obvious candidates from their personal networks and preferred reading. However, in these particular instances, women writers, myself included, stepped forward to explain that we had indeed been approached to contribute, in an effort to secure gender balance but we were already over-committed and simply could not find the time. When any group is under-represented in a wider population, individuals in that group can and do find themselves called on more often than they can easily accommodate by those acting with the best of motives.

One all too frequent example of the burden of 'good citizenship' in SF & Fantasy circles is the amount of writing time female authors lose when some article claiming, for example, that women's voices are missing from Science Fiction (Zebedee, 2016), is published and widely shared online. Or when articles in the mainstream media about epic fantasy (Walter, 2008, 2011, 2013), prompted by a new series of Game of Thrones, conspicuously fail to mention a single female author. Every such article hands women writers a poisonous choice. We can object, with all the hassles and loss of our own working time which that presenting evidence to the contrary will entail, as well as dealing the usual counter-objections, ugly insults and even threats. Or we can let the erasure stand, damaging women in SF&F, present and future.

This double-edged sword becomes all the sharper when such activities are specifically related to gender issues. Women most often take on responsibility for monitoring and investigating discrimination and related issues, and are even expected to do this, because they are the ones most directly affected by any workplace bias. Yet their findings are invariably undermined, however subtly or unconsciously, by a supposed predisposition among women or any minority group to argue their own most favourable case. Put simply, 'she would say that, wouldn't she? Because she's the one who will benefit from change.' Male-authored reports on equality and diversity issues carry far more weight. In the SF & F genre, we can be accordingly thankful for writers such as John Scalzi who tackle this with articles such as 'Straight White Male: The Lowest Difficulty Setting There Is' (Scalzi, 2012).

Another aspect of the Sticky Floor that's been widely identified is the persistence of all or male-dominated conferences and discussion panels across all industries, professions and disciplines. There is a Tumblr account (Allmalepanels 2015-ongoing) dedicated to highlighting these, illustrating the breadth and extent of this problem. Similar panels have long been a feature of SF & Fantasy conventions. These events are volunteer and fan run and as such are particularly vulnerable to the influence of Affinity Groups, a problem long identified in many areas of professional recruitment. When the Halo Effect predisposes someone to work with people like them, when they are asked to think of someone with the knowledge or skills required for a particular project, their first thoughts will be drawn from the group of people they know and whose track record they trust. Notable examples of Affinity Grouping in SF & Fantasy film and TV are the 'repertory companies' of actors whom Christopher Nolan and Joss Whedon call on, time and again. As these examples show, Affinity Grouping is not of itself inevitably sexist or racist, but studies of its effects in recruitment have shown it leads to people in positions of authority gathering teams predominately drawn from their own gender and ethnic group.

Where women do participate in conventions, they are

still frequently and persistently grouped in discussions limiting their participation to debating gender issues. At the 2011 World Fantasy Convention in San Diego, women writers who could have offered valuable opinions on a range of writing topics were allocated to 'Breaking the Crystal Ceiling'. At the World Fantasy Convention in 2013, I was one of the women authors whose sole panel was 'Broads with Swords', supposedly inviting us to wonder if women can actually write epic fantasy? Across the whole gamut of SF conventions, women and writers of colour have historically been woefully under-represented as Guests of Honour.

Since 2012 there has been a movement towards more diversity among guests and panel parity within SF & Fantasy events, prompted by a couple of now-notorious comic industry events, Mark Millar's Kapow! Comic Con (About a Grrrl, 2012) and London Super Comic Con, where organisers claimed they simply couldn't find women to take part. Fan and creator outrage soon followed and things have improved slightly. As Chair of the 2013 Eastercon in Bradford, UK, I worked with a committee absolutely committed to gender parity across the event (Bradshaw, 2012). With a membership and a programme volunteer pool that was gender balanced and included a good number of writers of colour, anything else was unthinkable.

Achieving this across a four-day programme of multiple streams took a considerable amount of work, given practical constraints such as avoiding programme clashes or times when a particular person wasn't available. Some items proved harder to assemble a panel for, either because fewer people were attending the convention with those particular interests, or because certain items (in particular, those with an element of performance, such as panel games) attract fewer volunteers. Nevertheless, we managed to do it across the convention as a whole by having as equal as possible a gender split on each item (Bradshaw, 2013).

Other conventions showing similar commitment include, but are by no means limited to, Bristolcon, British FantasyCon and Nineworlds Geekfest. However, since conventions are volunteer-led events such policies remain entirely voluntary and some convention committees have no hesitation in dismissing panel parity as unnecessary. This is frequently on the basis of 'we want the best people available' which inevitably ends up implying that the best people are still somehow more likely to be male, because they dominate the subsequent line-up. Such attitudes have no basis in logic or statistical analysis of convention attendees.

Thankfully, recent research across a wide range of industries and disciplines has demonstrated that a more gender-balanced and diverse workforce brings direct, tangible benefits to companies and professions. It ushers in new perspectives to help solve problems, finds ways to appeal and to serve a far wider customer base, and expands into profitable new markets across increasingly diverse populations. As has so often been the case in discussions of equality, once the commercial case can be made, change follows more swiftly.

Similarly, in SF & Fantasy, those conventions which opt to secure panel parity find that the introduction of new and diverse voices, offering new perspectives and raising new questions, benefits the whole event which in turn benefits the wider genre community. The 2013 Eastercon has been widely praised as offering a very high standard of interesting and varied programming. To quote one middle-aged, white male author who came up to me in the Green Room, to ask me as Chair to congratulate the committee, 'I've really enjoyed my panels. It's not been the same old people saying the same old things!' LGBT authors and those of colour also enjoyed being able to talk about their work rather than 'their struggle' yet again.

The fact remains, though, that until panel parity becomes the norm across SF & Fantasy conventions, this ongoing lack of proportionate visibility for women, writers of colour and others will continue to contribute to the Sticky Floor phenomenon.

The Leaky Pipeline

Those writers who do escape it must now face the Leaky Pipeline. This describes the way that women drop out of particular careers in greater numbers than men, at each successive stage. Various reasons for this have been identified, across a range of disciplines and professions.

The persistence of the gender pay gap is one such reason, itself a consequence of women being hampered by the sticky floor. If you cannot progress in an organisation, you won't get the financial rewards of promotion. There is also the problem of cultural pressures making women far less likely to negotiate for a higher payment than that which is initially offered. Does this apply to authors, given that writers are in effect independent contractors rather than employees within a hierarchy?

There is certainly evidence of a gender pay gap for writers, as established by the 2015 report *The Business of Being an Author: A Survey of Authors Earnings and Contracts* (Gibson, Johnson and Dimita, 2015), commissioned by the Authors' Licensing and Collecting Society (ALCS), with research carried out by Queen Mary University of London. This report established that a significant gender pay gap amongst professional authors of fiction, women's earnings are 80% of earnings by men. This gap is much greater than in the population as a whole where women earn 91.5% of male earnings. It is only when income from all forms of writing is assessed, including script writing, technical, non-fiction and other publishing, that the gender pay gap shrinks.

This report also established that authors' earnings are declining across the board, for men and women alike. It is increasingly difficult to make a living as an author, irrespective of gender or other factors. However, this gender pay gap means that sustaining a full-time writing career as a novelist becomes financially impossible for women sooner and in greater numbers, than it does for their male counterparts.

Across industry, academia and in nearly all professions, the point at which most women leave is when they start a family. The costs of childcare are cited as the decisive factor in numerous studies. Faced with such demands, the lowest earner in a couple will be the one who leaves work. Given the persistence of wage inequalities, that lowest earner is most likely to be the woman. This calculation will apply to writers just as much as any other group. A full-time writer may not leave formal employment but if childcare outside the home is unaffordable, time previously spent on writing will now be lost.

But surely authors can work flexibly, offering opportunities to continue working which employees with fixed hours cannot access? This is certainly true, and male and female writers alike manage to fit in their writing around their families while a higher-earning spouse goes out to work. This mirrors research in other areas which indicates access to flexible working enables parents to continue in a chosen career rather than dropping out, such as the 2016 Bar Standards Report on Women at the Bar, considering this issue in relation to legal careers in the UK.

Progress has certainly been made across the board when it comes to an equal gender distribution of practical household tasks like cleaning and ironing, and taking care of children. As a growing number of men demand flexible working to counter the stresses of achieving a work-life balance, these realities of modern life are becoming more newsworthy and thus more widely discussed as more than 'women's issue' (Espiner, 2017). But gender related factors must still be considered, particularly in relation to the creative industries. When it comes to the mental effort of running a household, of managing a family's schedules, making sure that necessary shopping is done, that bills are paid on time and all such other intangible demands, women still bear the heaviest burden (Valenti, 2015).

When time and mental space are needed to produce a writer's best work, women authors who are parents are going to be more frequently disadvantaged than men. This is the reality, not 'nappy brain' which is frequently merely a veiled reworking of the old misogynistic notion that motherhood somehow renders a woman less mentally fit, less committed, less suited to pursuing a career. Indeed, as two-career households and an equal sharing of practical household tasks become the norm, new fathers and their employers alike are discovering that the effects of parental sleep-deprivation and the burden of a whole new set of responsibilities and obligations are the same irrespective of gender (PRC, 2015).

This becomes particularly relevant to writing when considering the annual cycle of publishing required to achieve and sustain a best-selling writing career over a period of years. If the demands of family life make it impossible for a writer, male or female, to deliver a novel to the expected standard to the required deadline, that author and that publisher will soon have a problem. 'Publish or perish' is a mantra that doesn't only apply to academic writing. An author who does not produce work on a regular basis will soon drop out of public view. The lists of books submitted for prizes such as the Arthur C Clarke Awards illustrate this (ACCA, 2016b). The names of authors that recur year in, year out, are overwhelmingly male.

This problem has been exacerbated by changes in retailing which mean that bookstores now rarely carry an author's backlist. In the UK, this change was driven from 2008 onwards by publishers deciding to cut their own costs by changing the terms on which they supplied stock to retailers. Rather than all titles being offered on sale or return, that would now only apply to books published within the previous 18 months. All older titles would be firm sale only. Retailers responded by simply opting not to stock these older books, not least because other commercial pressures were encouraging them to try diversification, stocking their limited shelf-space with other products such as stationery or games.

When an author's backlist is not routinely stocked, their sales will go down. No online retailer has managed to replicate the pattern of browsing and impulse purchases which bookstores have always fostered. As a title's sales go down, it moves ever closer to the red line in a publisher's accounts below which reprinting is no longer considered commercially viable. As this trend accelerates, the end result is that the book goes out of print. As an author's sales decline, they are less likely to able to secure new publishing contracts or if they can, their advances will be lower. None of these commercial considerations are directly discriminatory but when the impact is greater for women, the indirect effects become so.

When considering visibility, women authors are consistently under-represented in those 'Best of the Year,' 'Best of All Time' 'Must-Read Genre Classics' lists which might otherwise prompt keen readers to ask booksellers to order titles which they cannot find on the shelves. Women authors who are earning less than their male counterparts will also have less money available to spend on boosting their work's visibility by going to SF & Fantasy conventions, especially when those events are outside their own country. Literary festivals still frequently do not pay anything more than minimal expenses at best. Once again, female authors will find it harder to justify spending time and money from their more limited resources on such self-promotional activities.

How easy is it for writers to make up such lost ground as children grow up and the demands on parents change? It seems likely that this is where an author's freelance status can work against them, as can be seen in other careers. The self-employed have none of the employment law protections designed to mitigate the impact of parental leave on full-time workers. In professions, such as the law in the UK, where freelancers and employed barristers work alongside each other, over 70% of those responding to the most recent Bar Society survey reported that parental leave had a negative impact on their career progression. Key issues mentioned were a loss of clients and contacts, and financial issues due to a drop in income. Case studies cited in this report quote freelancers far more often than employed barristers. Certainly authors who are parents, who cannot afford to go to conventions or publishing events, will have far fewer chances to maintain professional contacts or to learn of new opportunities. The same is obviously true for those with other caring responsibilities, a group once again predominately female.

Another widely cited explanation for Leaky Pipe losses of women staff is harassment. Across all industries and professions, 60% of women report unwanted sexual advances, verbal and physical, as well as other instances of workplace bullying. Black and minority ethnic respondents to such surveys report harassment in significantly higher rates than white colleagues. While the trend in recent years indicates that such harassment is decreasing somewhat, the problem still remains substantial. Despite the increasing enforcement of anti-discrimination legislation, only a minority of those who report harassment when responding to surveys take formal action in the workplace. Complainants feel, often with good reason, that they won't be believed, that they will be considered troublemakers, or that they will be the ones to suffer repercussions, particularly when there is a significant imbalance of influence and status between themselves and the offender.

Reluctance to report incidents for similar reasons, and the difficulty of surveying a widely scattered group of freelancers such as authors make it very difficult to assess the extent of in-person harassment in SF & Fantasy. However there are sufficient and recurrent high-profile incidents to indicate such a problem exists. Readercon's banning of Rene Walling (Glyer, 2012) and Wiscon's banning of Jim Frenkel (Glyer, 2014) are merely two such examples from the SF & Fantasy convention circuit. There is no reason to suppose that such things do not contribute to the loss of women writers from the profession.

Online harassment is a visibly growing problem for women authors and writers of colour. Theodore Beale (Vox Day)'s attack on award-winning African-American author N. K. Jemisin is a prime example of such racist and sexist abuse. In this instance, misuse of the organisation's resources enabled SFWA to expel him from their membership (Locus, 2013), but as Beale's subsequent antics show, such as his support for the 'Gamergate' hate campaigns focused on women in the computer game industry, it remains appallingly easy for abusers to target individuals through social media.

To say that these targets should just shrug off deeply personal, vile threats and insults by 'not feeding the trolls' or by 'just' using the mute and block buttons is to misunderstand crucial aspects of this problem. The issue is not merely hurt feelings, though surely everyone should have the right to go about their lives and work without being bombarded with gratuitous insults? When considering the direct impact of abuse on writers' careers, the sheer time it takes to block and mute hundreds of constantly morphing and relentless accounts can and does run into tens if not hundreds of hours. Being the target of a sustained online hate campaign also massively disrupts an author's online relationship with their established fans and potential new readers. This should be likened to a DDOS attack on a company's website.

Of course, men experience online harassment, often to an appalling extent. Just as they face bias and prejudice in daily life, up to and including sexism. However where male and female experience of harassment differs is in the frequency, intensity and context of such attacks. Where online interaction plays a more significant role for women authors, LGBT writers and those of colour, derailing and silencing harassment will have a proportionately greater impact.

For example, when women writers whose early titles have gone out of print choose to independently publish those works as e-books, online self-promotion is vital. The same is true for small presses which publish work deemed too 'minority interest' to gain publicity in the mainstream media or widespread distribution through bookshops. The impact here goes beyond diversity considerations to direct commercial impacts when one considers how many recent prize-winning and shortlisted 'breakout' books have come from small presses, where so much new talent is currently nurtured (Sullivan, 2016). Examples include but are not limited to *The Testament of Jessie Lamb* by Jane Rogers,

Arthur C Clarke Award winner 2012, first published by Sandstone Press, and *His Bloody Project* by Graeme Macrae Burnet, Booker Prize shortlisted and published by the Contraband imprint of Saraband Books.

As women get older, 'social invisibility' becomes an issue leading to them leaving careers in a great many fields. Once again, there is no reason to assume that SF & Fantasy is in any way immune to this particular manifestation of the Leaky Pipe. Even events run with the very best of intentions can fall into this trap. The first Nine World Geekfest in 2013 sought to promote new and diverse voices within SF & Fantasy, alongside a roster of best-selling authors to draw attendance to this new event. When the programme was finalised, the absence of female authors over forty was noticeable. I was one of a handful of those who had initially been approached to participate, only to be told that our presence could no longer be accommodated when the final programme was drawn up. There was no deliberate intent to exclude us but the indirectly discriminatory effect remained, since that roster of best-sellers deemed essential to draw a crowd turned out to be predominately male.

The Glass Ceiling

This brings us to the final challenge identified by workplace surveys of gender issues: the Glass Ceiling. In publishing, the top tier of best-selling writers remains dominated by men, even while the presence of best-selling women makes it plain that masculinity is not a pre-requisite for such success. Top-tier status is determined purely by sales, so there can be no overt discrimination at work, as can still be found in corporate boardrooms and academic institutions.

However, this is where we see that the Glass Ceiling for authors is the end result of the cumulative and successive indirect discrimination that has been examined thus far. As long as successful male authors are more easily able to sustain their careers with a regular annual flow of books, they are less likely to lose that privileged position. While disparate factors combine to make progression up through the ranks of authors more difficult for women, and for LGBT individuals and people of colour, the chances of a white, western male writer securing one of the few top spots that become vacant are accordingly enhanced.

When considering the careers of best-selling authors, across all genres and regardless of gender, the importance of the 'breakout book' becomes apparent. It also becomes immediately obvious that this is seldom if ever a writer's first book. Authors are made, not born. It takes sustained practise and experience to hone an author's skills to the point where they write that 'breakout' story. Where disparate and indirectly discriminatory factors combine to deny such practise and experience to women, LGBT authors and writers of colour, their chances of such a 'breakout' publication are correspondingly reduced.

Conclusion

So what conclusions should we draw? Should writers without the inherent advantages of white masculinity simply throw in the towel? Of course not. Any writer with a good story to share and a distinctive voice to tell it should go for it whatever their background! It is self-evidently possible to build a writing career as a woman, as an author of colour, as a LGBT individual. Those lists of books recommended for 2017 cited at the start of this paper make that abundantly clear. The ups and downs of male authors' careers, outlined in countless blogs, make it equally apparent that success for anyone is an achievement against the odds. They may be playing 'Writer' on the lowest difficulty setting but this is still a very difficult game.

However it is important for all those with an interest in the SF & Fantasy genre, in publishing, retail, writing and fandom, to recognise indirect discrimination exists, just as it does in other industries, professions and disciplines. Studies have also shown that such indirect discrimination is cumulative. As those industries, professions and disciplines have explored the reasons for their own gender disparities, they have recognised that legislation, policies and procedures designed to prevent direct discrimination are not enough to solve these problems. It is now widely agreed that businesses and professional organisations should work to actively mitigate the indirect discriminatory effects of wider business, social and cultural factors, as far as they possibly can and that such initiatives must be intersectional. The Science Fiction & Fantasy genre can do the same. Quite apart from anything else, it makes commercial sense for everyone involved.

Bibliography

About a Grrrl, 2012. *Women in Comics: Kapow! No Women at Cons.* [online] Available at: < http://www.comicbookgrrrl.com/2012/02/14/women-in-comics-kapow-no-women-at-cons> [Accessed 17 January 2017].

ACCA, 2016. *Award Winners.* [online] Available at: < https://www.clarkeaward.com/award-winners> [Accessed 17 January 2017].

ACCA, 2016b. *The Arthur C Clarke Award. 2016 Submissions List.* [online] Available at: < https://www.clarkeaward.com/2016-submission-list> [Accessed 17 January 2017].

Allmalepanels, 2015-2017. *Congrats, you have an all male panel!* [online] Available at: < http://allmalepanels.tumblr.com> [Accessed 17 January 2017].

Bar Standards Board, 2016. *Women at the Bar.* [online] Available at: <https://www.barstandardsboard.org.uk/media/1773934/women_at_the_bar_-_full_report_-_final_12_07_16.pdf> [Accessed 17 January 2017].

Bates, L., 2014. *Everyday Sexism.* [online] Available at: <http://everydaysexism.com> [Accessed 17 January 2017].

Bradshaw, S.J., 2012. *Why we are committing to Gender Parity on Panels.* [online] Available at: < https://eightsquaredcon.wordpress.com/2012/04/27/why-we-are-committing-to-gender-parity-on-panels> [Accessed 17 January 2017].

Bradshaw, S.J., 2013. *Panel Parity – what we achieved, and how we did it.* [online] Available at: < https://eightsquaredcon.wordpress.com/2013/05/06/panel-parity-what-we-achieved-and-how-we-did-it> [Accessed 17 January 2017].

Book View Cafe, 2012-2017. [online] Available at: < http://bookviewcafe.com/bookstore/about-book-view-cafe> [Accessed 17 January 2017].

Broad Universe, 2015-2017. [online] Available at: <https://broaduniverse.org> [Accessed 17 January 2017].

Catwoman, 2004. [film] Directed by Pitof. USA: Warner Bros.

Correll, S.J., 2004. *Constraints into Preferences: Gender, Status, and Emerging Career Aspirations*. [online] Available at: < http://people.uncw.edu/maumem/soc500/Correll2004.pdf> [Accessed 17 January 2017].

Cosh, E.G., 2016. *The 2015 SF Count*. [online] Available at: < http://strangehorizons.com/non-fiction/articles/the-2015-sf-count> [Accessed 17 January 2017].

Cosh, E.G., 2016b. *The 2015 SF Count*. [online] Available at: < http://strangehorizons.com/non-fiction/articles/the-2015-sf-count> [Accessed 17 January 2017].

Cunningham, J., 2017. *96 Books Sci-Fi & Fantasy Editors Can't Wait for You to Read in 2017*. [online] Available at: < http://www.barnesandnoble.com/blog/sci-fi-fantasy/96-books-sci-fi-fantasy-editors-cant-wait-for-you-to-read-in-2017> [Accessed 17 January 2017].

Daredevil, 2003. [film] Directed by Mark Steven Johnson. USA: Marvel Enterprises.

Dubois-Shaik, F. and Fusulier, B. eds., 2015. *Academic Careers and Gender Inequality: Leaky Pipeline and Interrelated Phenomena in Seven European Countries*. [online] Available at: <http://garciaproject.eu/wp-content/uploads/2015/11/GARCIA_report_wp5D.pdf> [Accessed 17 January 2017].

Elektra, 2005. [film] Directed by Rob Bowman. USA: Twentieth Century Fox.

Ellemers, N., Van den Heuvel, H., De Gilder, D., Maass, A. and Bonvini, A., 2004. The underrepresentation of women in science: Differential commitment or the queen bee syndrome? *British Journal of Social Psychology*, 43:1-24.

Espiner, T., 2017. *Work-life balance 'increasingly stressful for fathers'*. [online] Available at: < http://www.bbc.co.uk/news/business-38607682> [Accessed 17 January 2017].

Gibson, J., Johnson, P. and Dimita, G., 2015. *The Business of Being an Author A Survey of Author's Earnings and Contracts*. [online] Available at: <https://www.alcs.co.uk/Documents/Final-Report-For-Web-Publication-(2).aspx> [Accessed 17 January 2017].

Glyer, M., 2012. *Readercon Bans René Walling for 2 Years*. [online]

Available at: < http://file770.com/?p=9777> [Accessed 17 January 2017].

Glyer, M., 2014. *Jim Frenkel Banned By Wiscon.* [online] Available at: <http://file770.com/?p=17948> [Accessed 17 January 2017].

Green Lantern, 2011. [film] Directed by Martin Campbell. USA: Warner Bros. Pictures.

Lawrence, M., 2016. *The Final Round of the Self-Published Fantasy Blog-Off 2016.* [online] Available at: < http://mark---lawrence.blogspot.co.uk/2016/08/the-final-round-of-self-published.html> [Accessed 17 January 2017].

Liptak, A., 2017. *33 science fiction and fantasy books that everyone will be talking about in 2017.* [online] Available at: < http://www.theverge.com/2017/1/5/13811144/sci-fi-fantasy-book-recommendations-2017> [Accessed 17 January 2017].

Locus, 2013. *SFWA Board Votes to Expel Beale.* [online] Available at: < http://www.locusmag.com/News/2013/08/beale-expelled-from-sfwa> [Accessed 17 January 2017].

Marr, A., 2016. *Sleuths, Spies and Sorcerers: Andrew Marr's Paperback Heroes.* [online] Available at: < http://www.bbc.co.uk/programmes/p04dz4xk> [Accessed 17 January 2017].

McKenna, J.E., 2014. *Waterstones & Gender Equality. The good, the bad & the business case for doing better.* [online] Available at: < http://www.julietemckenna.com/?p=1352> [Accessed 17 January 2017].

Nichols, C., 2015. *Homme de Plume: What I Learned Sending My Novel Out Under a Male Name.* [online] Available at: < http://jezebel.com/homme-de-plume-what-i-learned-sending-my-novel-out-und-1720637627> [Accessed 17 January 2017].

PRC, 2015. *Raising Kids and Running a Household: How Working Parents Share the Load.* [online] Available at: < http://www.pewsocialtrends.org/2015/11/04/raising-kids-and-running-a-household-how-working-parents-share-the-load> [Accessed 17 January 2017].

RSE, 2012. *Tapping all our Talents. Women in science, technology, engineering and mathematics: a strategy for Scotland.* [online] Available at: <http://www.rse.org.uk/wp-content/uploads/2016/10/tapping_talents.pdf> [Accessed 17 January 2017].

Scalzi, J., 2012. *Straight White Male: The Lowest Difficulty Setting There Is*. [online] Available at: <http://whatever.scalzi.com/2012/05/15/straight-white-male-the-lowest-difficulty-setting-there-is> [Accessed 17 January 2017].

SFWA, 2013. *Nebula Awards Winners Announced.* [online] Available at: < http://www.sfwa.org/2014/05/2013-nebula-awards-winners> [Accessed 17 January 2017].

SFWA, 2017. *SFWA Board. Officers: July 1st, 2016 to June 30th, 2017.* [online] Available at: < http://www.sfwa.org/about/current-officers> [Accessed 17 January 2017].

Smeding, A., 2012. *Women in Science, Technology, Engineering, and Mathematics (STEM): An Investigation of Their Implicit Gender Stereotypes and Stereotypes' Connectedness to Math Performance.* [online] Available at: < http://link.springer.com/article/10.1007/s11199-012-0209-4> [Accessed 17 January 2017].

Sullivan, K., 2016. *The poaching game.* [online] Available at: < http://www.thebookseller.com/blogs/poaching-game-412561> [Accessed 17 January 2017].

Valenti, J., 2015. *Men think they do equal work at home, when facts show otherwise.* [online] Available at: < https://www.theguardian.com/commentisfree/2015/nov/09/men-only-pull-their-weight-at-home-in-a-world-where-thinking-doesnt-matter> [Accessed 17 January 2017].

Van den Brink, M. and Benschop, Y., 2012. Slaying the Seven-Headed Dragon: The Quest for Gender Change in Academia. *Gender, Work and Organization,* Vol. 19 No 1.

VIDA, 2012. *About the VIDA count.* [online] Available at: < http://www.vidaweb.org/the-count> [Accessed 17 January 2017].

Walter, D., 2008. *Take a break somewhere fantastic.* [online] Available at: < http://www.theguardian.com/books/booksblog/2008/may/30/takeabreaksomewherefantast> [Accessed 17 January 2017].

Walter, D., 2011. *George RR Martin's fantasy is not far from reality.* [online] Available at: < http://www.theguardian.com/books/2011/jul/26/george-r-r-martin-fantasy-reality> [Accessed 17 January 2017].

Walter, D., 2013. *There's more to fantasy than the elves and orcs of Tolkien.* [online] Available at: < http://www.theguardian.com/books/

booksblog/2013/oct/11/fantasy-novel-elves-orcs-tolkien> [Accessed 17 January 2017].

West, D., Jacquet, J., King, M.M., Correll, S.J. and Bergstrom, C.T., 2013. *The Role of Gender in Scholarly Authorship*. [online] Available at: <http://journals.plos.org/plosone/article?id=10.1371/journal.pone.0066212> [Accessed 17 January 2017].

Zebedee, J., 2016. *Women: Missing Voices In Science Fiction*. [online] Available at: < http://booksbywomen.org/women-missing-voices-in-science-fiction-by-jo-zebebee> [Accessed 17 January 2017].

Bikini Armour: women characters, readers and writers in male narratives

By Anna Milon

This essay owes its title to the blog www.bikiniarmourbattledamage. tumblr.com, whose writers poke fun at the unrealistic and often downright hazardous female 'armour' in various franchises. I have chosen the title for two reasons: firstly, to highlight hypersexualisation and the demand for physical prowess, the rock and hard place between which fantasy heroines are often caught; secondly, because, like the impractical armour, narratives that we female readers expect to protect us often turn against us.

Fantasy, because of its setting in a remote past (albeit an imaginary one), and its roots in male-centred narratives, is often not expected to challenge gender inequality and lack of representation. Because 'that's just how things were back in the day'. And yet it is a genre exponentially growing in popularity. That and fantasy literature's association with a young demographic: children and teenagers – forces an uncomfortable question of what exactly are we teaching our children.

Drawing on a wide range of gender criticism of modern fantasy literature and conducting close reading comparisons between male-coded and female-coded protagonists, I shall navigate the temptations, as female reader and writer, of buying into the false security of the male epic and discuss whether there is such a thing as 'the female gaze'.

Sophia McDougal criticises 'the patronising promise of a strong female character' (2013), because such characters are anomalies juxtaposed to the male 'strong' default, and because they are measured according to physicality, not according to their complexity as individuals. She is echoed by Tania Modleski, who writes of the double standard that validates male narratives as 'important' and dismisses female narratives as 'trivial' (2007). Although women are permitted into male heroic narratives of warfare, they are marked out as alien. 'War is the province of men' (Jackson, 2003)[1] and 'battles are ugly when women fight' (Lewis, 1998:72). In order to fit in, a woman needs to obscure her femininity in pursuit of the male ideal. But being in a heroic narrative does not make her any less woman. This case of mimicry may seem to provide a degree of control, as we play a double game of performing both for the male gaze, as sexual objects, and as the male gaze, subscribing to the dominant social order. However, Diane Negra writes that post-feminism 'fetishizes female power and desire while consistently placing these within firm limits' (2009:4). These limits are dictated by the dominant (patriarchal) social order. 'Strong female character' becomes shorthand for a sexually available heroine that enacts a male role, but is happy to blend in with the wallpaper once she meets her intended true love, who is of course a man. Male power thus remains the *modus operandi*. Sex is seen as the ultimate solution for women: 'many men [believe that] if we are free with sex we are truly liberated, and our identity problems are gone' (Salzman-Webb, 1971:15-16). But being in charge of one's sexuality is something still firmly rooted in the male narrative. Although the alpha-female (also known as 'the warrior princess'), 'usually pictured with a weapon, a gigantic schlonglike weapon – is a character infused with

---

1. Director Peter Jackson in *The Lord of the Rings: The Return of the King*, based on the eponymous work by J. R. R. Tolkien.

power, sexuality, confidence, and ass-kicking prowess' (Wendel and Tan, 2009:58), but she still belongs to the male narrative, 'only when embracing the moral and character strengths of heroes can a woman embrace her sex drive as well' (ibid). The female identity and sexuality remain defined by men. This is evident in the common policing of female supernatural powers by male authority in fantasy fiction. In Leigh Bardugo's *Grisha* trilogy (2012-2014), Alina can only access her Sun-summoner powers when in direct physical contact with the Darkling, though others with similar powers need no such special conditions. In both the *Infernal Devices* (Clare, 2010-2013) and *Worldmaker* (Hounsom, 2015-2017) trilogies young women are forced into cooperating with organisations intent on exploiting their powers, as well as male figures pursuing the same goal. Equally, the 'happily ever after' ending sees female characters 'at the very least, domesticated' (Modleski, 2007:12): the princess is married, the shield-maiden rediscovers her nurturing side, the shrew is tamed. Fantasy fiction is dominated by conventions of the male heroic, in which women have a place only as subjects.

Rosemary Jackson presents fantasy fiction as fundamentally transgressive and challenging to the social order in which it is created, and yet in some aspects it remains staunchly normative, perhaps owing to the need to be 'so close to the real that you almost have to believe in it' (1981:27). Gender roles are one of the aspects anchoring fantasy in the familiar and the 'real'. Since fantasy is largely set in a historic past or its fictional alternatives, misogyny is often not questioned because 'that's just how things were back then'. It may be argued that the genre of fantasy presupposes gender inequality because its origins are inherently sexist. The medieval courtly romance and the works of J. R. R. Tolkien are often cited as the inceptors of modern fantasy literature. Both have been scrutinised extensively for their treatment of female characters. Although courtly romance gave rise to such universally recognised figures as the questing knight and the damsel in distress, it presents a much wider array of characters of both sexes. Women 'of highe and lowe'[2] (Hahn, 1995:406) (of both high and low social standing) are acknowledged as having diverse wants, the chief among which is sovereignty over men: 'We desyren of men above alle maner thing,/ To have soverenyte' (422-423). In the particular case quoted, sovereignty is granted to the speaker, Dame Ragnelle, by her newly-wed husband, Sir Gawain:

> *I putt the choyse in you.*
> *Bothe body and godes, hartt, and every dele,*
> *Ys alle your oun, for to by and selle.*
>
> *I place the choice in your hands.*
> *Both body and possessions, heart, and every thing*
> *Is all your own, to buy or to sell.* (681-683)

At these words Dame Ragnelle, who was previously as ugly as an owl, transforms into the fairest lady at King Arthur's court. Although this transformation moves Ragnelle from her transgressive state as an unattractive single woman to the confines of beauty and married life, she

---

[2]. 'The Wedding of Sir Gawain and Dame Ragnelle'.

retains some control over her husband, who 'as a coward […] lay by her bothe day and nyghte' (808). The editor of the romance glosses this line as 'lay by her submissively'. Heroines of romance take charge of their sexuality as they woo knights who have captured their fancy. In *Amis and Amiloun* Belisaunt at first fails to persuade her paramour Amis to have an affair with her. She then threatens to accuse Amis of raping her, to 'say with michel wrong/ With strengthe thou hast me todrawe'[3] (Foster, 2007:633-634), unless he agrees to sleep with her. Execution by hanging is named as the punishment for rape. The incident indicates the value assigned to victims' voices (noble ones, at least), and the possibility of a woman admitting of having been raped without permanent damage to her reputation. While romance heroines are placed in an unambiguously patriarchal society, they are also given individual voices and a power to gain control without resorting to physical violence. Similarly, in Tolkien's works women are few, but they are presented as agents of their own fates. Eowyn openly challenges the conventions of womanhood:

> *All your words are but to say: you are a woman, and your part is in the house. But when the men have died in battle and honour, you have leave to be burned in the house, for the men will need it no more.* (2007:784)

She riles against the social constraints that conceive women as powerless. So does Arwen, who understands the

---

3. 'Amis and Amiloun'.

consequences of her choice to stay in Middle-Earth after her kin had departed for the Undying Lands, but who makes the decision and bears the consequence unflinchingly. All the female characters mentioned above engage in meaningful work: they set a personal goal and achieve it within the narrative, rather than being ornamental or instrumental to male designs.

To reach the happy ending that the teleological drive of these narratives presupposes, the women need to eventually be re-situated in society. That society being patriarchal, the heroines can only occupy positions of subordinates, a limited number of socially acceptable female roles. The highly formalised social roles of romance heroines especially are both a blessing and a curse. A curse because they considerably limit female activity in the narrative and reinforce gender stereotypes regarding 'appropriate' behaviour. But a blessing because those roles are superficial. Crystabel, the paramour of *Sir Eglamour*'s eponymous knight, falls pregnant by him; but, being separated from her lover and unable to reveal their illicit union, she is exiled from her father's house. After many trials and tribulations, separation from her child and the elapse of fifteen years, Crystabel is at the court of her uncle, who is ignorant of her fall from grace. There, she presents herself as a wronged maiden and is accepted as such. Tournaments are held for her hand in marriage (an honour reserved for young virginal women of high status) even though by that time she is approaching forty years of age. She plays the role of 'virgin' without ever being interrogated as to its validity. The narrator does not flag her behaviour as suspect and describes her in the same terms that are used to describe nubile brides-to-be.

The descriptions of romance beauties in general are highly formulaic: authors compare their whiteness to foam or lilies and claim that 'a feyrer thing of flesche ne fell/ was none in Christianite'[4] (Hudson, 2006:29-30), but they hardly ever address the actual appearance of the character. Is she thin or chubby? Athletic or curvaceous? Freckled? The title of 'the most beautiful woman in the world' simply signifies that this is the woman the protagonist will marry, not a measurement of her personal attributes. In fact, the same epithets that are used to describe women are applied to men in romance. These formulae act as metaphorical armour for heroines that signify their place in society much like physical armour situates an individual as a warrior. Both serve the purpose of concealment, and linguistic conventions do a much better job at protecting female identity than a chainmail bralette.

The trouble with many modern works of fantasy literature is that somewhere along the way those formulaic stereotypes of womanly perfection became internalised. Heroines, and by extent the readers who identify with them, are expected to conform to the 'contemporary hyper-thin European ideal of beauty' (Younger, 2003:47) regardless of their ethnicity. As white is the default race in many fantasy novels, thin is the default body type. And if a female character is explicitly written as anything other than borderline anorexic, artwork and adaptations often ignore the descriptions. For instance, Neil Gaiman (2001) describes Easter as voluptuous, her thighs rubbing together as she walks, yet Kristin Chenoweth cast to portray her in the upcoming television adaptation purportedly weighs 45kg at 4 feet 11 inches tall. Apart

---

4. 'Sir Eglamour of Artois'.

from demonstrating the 'appropriate' weight and beauty standards, female protagonists coach their readers in self-assessment and self-policing.

For many young women controlling [weight] provides a sense of power, but that sense of power is false, since deliberately reducing one's body size usually diminishes physical strength (Younger, 2003:51).

Younger argues that 'female power, sexual and otherwise, is connected to a thin, lean body' (52). Being thin is, of course, bound to the warrior-princess image. For women in Western society thin equals fit. Considering the current masculinised beauty standards: narrow hips, flat chests – the 'thin, lean body' women are encouraged to aspire to is the male body. Moreover, an overwhelming majority of mentors in fantasy are men. While learning fencing, minstrelsy and horse-riding, or progressing on their quest, the protagonist also observes a male role-model. No one teaches heroines how to be female. On the other hand, there is a wealth of male characters who raise or educate young girls: Theoden and Eowyn, Geralt of Rivia and Ciri, the Darkling and Alina. But the male gaze does not allow the heroine to blend seamlessly into her milieu as long as she retains her sexuality, an integral part of her identity. Thus, the author is coaxed into telling the story of a woman in relation to male desire. And 'telling implies using the language of the dominant order and so accepting its norms' (Jackson, 1981:4).

However, the shallowness of strong female characters cannot be solely caused by women writers who cannot write, as Joanna Russ would have it, but due to readers who cannot read. We live in a patriarchy and in patriarchies the female culture occupies 'a small corner of what we think of officially as possible human experience. Both men *and women* in our culture conceive the culture from a single point of view – the male' (Russ, 1995:81). While a writer can actively shun the dominant cultural myths in favour of creating believable female stories, will the readers be able to recognise these narratives? The interpretive community towards which fantasy fiction is marketed is so heavily steeped in the male heroic that it accepts the male viewpoint as the only feasibility, regardless of the protagonists' gender. L-J. Baker's *Promises, Promises* is a curious experiment in which the author, whose style belies her as a reader rather than a writer of fantasy, replaces the customarily male protagonists of a sword and sorcery narrative with three women. Written as a parody, it pushes characters to be vocal about misogyny and class issues that are generally omitted from fantasy narratives, attempting to subvert the male heroic. Or so I thought until I encountered the Amazon with 'flaming red hair and breasts barely restrained in a skimpy leather bra with aggressive conical metal points over the nipples' (Baker, 2013:64). As if that were not enough, she also sports 'a pair of utterly inadequate chainmail panties' (64). While the characters are critical of 'men's stranglehold on the definition of sex roles' (66), the narrative does nothing to challenge them. Out of the three female protagonists, two are at least partially male-coded. 'Sandy' could be short for 'Alexander' as well as 'Sandra', and her preoccupation with getting laid and the physical attributes of her potential partners smacks more of a teenage boy than a 24-year-old woman. Drusilla is never seen without her paring knife, which, true to its phallic connotations, she presents as an extension of herself. The only traditionally feminine protagonist, Ruth, is described as quiet and 'plain, easily-overlooked young woman' (30). The pageant-worthy string of candidates for the role of romantic interest are identified by the whiteness of their skin, the colour of their eyes and the cuteness of their pout. Sandy's offhand surprise that 'acne alone is not responsible for [Drusilla's] lack of girl action' (37) introduces the need for women to police their appearance and to hold it precedent over their personality regardless of their sexual orientation. Amidst the caricatures of buxom amazons and feisty grannies *Promises, Promises* offers no convincing female characters to identify with. It is a textbook example of changing the gender of a character and assuming the experience, apart from superficial details like period cramps, to be the same. And that is not good enough.

If 'our literature is not about women, […] it is by and about men' (Russ, 1995:81), in order for a female character to be portrayed faithfully to herself and to her author, her story is a struggle first and a journey second. It is necessarily 'the formation of an inner drive toward the assertion of selfhood in resistance to the overt and violating male plots of ambition' (Brooks, 1992:39). But, as has been claimed by scholars from Tolkien to Jackson, fantasy is a vehicle of escape. In many cases, an escape from the struggle of asserting the female voice, from striving to be heard. For women readers identifying with the dominant position[5] offers them a taste of power without the necessity to subvert the existing social order. By adopting the male gaze, such

---

5. The male position, although it can be occupied by a character of any gender.

readers are able to dissociate themselves from the 'female subject' that occupies a traditional feminine role. Women readers are consistently punished for seeking out characters who are like themselves. Fantasy heroines are too often superhuman, not by virtue of being Starborn, or a Shadowhunter, or the brightest witch of their generation, but because they represent unattainable perfection. Where male protagonists are often everyman figures, their female counterparts are ideals to aspire to. When female readers try to write a figure to identify with into their favourite narrative, such attempts are labelled Mary-Sues, self-insertions, and scorned. Real women have no place in stories.

When I began drafting this essay, I subtitled it 'projection and protecting female identity'. Projection, in this case, is the superficial imitation of a character or persona in everyday situations, such as cosplay, or identifying with a book or film character to the extent of adopting their mannerisms. As well as acting, projecting involves an element of self-persuasion. Like heroines who are written from the male point of view, women are encouraged to fit into the patriarchal narratives of our society. Since female roles are largely submissive, women are also guided towards adopting male roles as a means of having agency. In an attempt to protect their selves from the objectifying male gaze, some women project a male persona as a buffer. This projection does not denounce the woman's biological sex or her female gender, but is best, in my opinion, expressed in the words of Joanna Russ: 'I had just changed into a man, me, Joanna. I mean the female man, of course; my body and soul were exactly the same' (1994:5). The mounting expectations to live up to the image of a 'strong, independent woman', yet not to seem an emasculating threat to men, results in a faulty logic. The thought process runs somewhat like this:

1. I identify as a female and am aware of my sexuality.
2. Being sexualised by others and regarded as a sexual object makes me uncomfortable.
3. Being objectified takes away my power and agency.
4. Men are the ones doing the objectifying because they occupy a dominant position.
5. If I imitate men in my behaviour, I will gain some of their power and agency.
6. It will let me take charge of my own sexuality because it is my choice to display it rather than a social demand.
7. I am more confident at being perceived as a sexual being.

Despite this elaborate internal monologue, the society's perception of the woman has not changed. Furthermore, she has consciously obstructed her own identity with a masculine mask, only to be more accepted by society that seeks to sexualise her.

A clear distinction must be made between gender dysphoria, the behaviour of agender or gender-fluid individuals, and projection. The latter is always subterfuge, a deception of self and others that does not affect the identity of the projector, only the way that identity is perceived. If a male persona is projected by a woman, it is tantamount to her trying to explain herself in (male) terms that society can understand. 'She is a Self trying to pretend that she is a different Self, one for whom her own self is Other.'

(Russ, 1994:85). This self-obliteration and self-abasement is considered the default female narrative mode (Modleski, 2007:13), the final stage in which the female readers are convinced that they, and the characters that represent them, are Other. Women readers seem to be prepared to objectify their sex, as L-J Baker does, and to obstruct their individuality in pursuit of male appraisal. Gender-bent versions of male characters are unrealistically curvaceous, scantily clad and completely unprotected from the objectifying gaze and enemy hordes alike. Gender-bent cosplay costumes, created by female fans, follow the same trend: tight bodices, heels and cleavage all serve to sexualise the wearer.

In a preface to *My Secret Garden* (1973), a collection of female sexual fantasies, Nancy puts her finger on a fundamental problem. Women, and women's fantasies, are too often seen in terms of *need*, not *want*. If a man believes a woman is satisfied (according to his own standards), then he also believes she does not need anything more. But fantasy, both in terms of an imaginary escapade and a fictional genre, is not a signifier of lack, but rather an addition to the daily experience. In fantasy fiction the divide between female need and male want is most clearly seen in the inception of the narratives. While for male characters the importance of free will and self-discovery is emphasised as they deliberate whether to set out on their quest; female characters are often forcibly displaced from their home environment. Even though the narrative dictates the hero's decision, he is described as making a choice which the heroine is denied. Frodo volunteers to take the One Ring into Mordor even though he could theoretically stay silent. But Kyndra, the protagonist of Lucy Hounsom's *Starborn* is forced to leave her ravaged hometown after its people almost murder her, believing her to be a demon. Furthermore, heroines are used to deconstruct the male heroic narrative. Kyndra muses:

> *Isn't that what you wished for? [...] A great adventure like the ones in your stories? But none of those stories ever mentioned the fear, the uncertainty or the homesickness. [...] She wasn't in a story.* (2015:128)

Once again, women do not belong in stories; but Hounsom's words take on a different edge: realistic female characters do not belong in male heroic narratives, and that much is true. Despite Joanna Russ's argument, quoted above, that positive cultural myths are overwhelmingly male, they are not exclusively male. There is no lack of historical female figures that held positions of power either by exploiting society's preconceptions of femininity or using methods that men have neglected. See *Princesses Behaving Badly* (McRobbie, 2013) or www.rejectedprincesses.com for a comprehensive list. However, the contents of the book and the way it is presented further show the entanglement of female power with the male heroic. While the contents feature women who have made morally questionable decisions throughout their lives, the cover features drawn vignettes of princesses drinking wine, kissing other women and beheading a man. Would a prince doing all those things be perceived as 'misbehaving'? Probably not. But these actions, that are perceived as 'hero' or 'macho' for men are inappropriate for women. Because the cover is the first aspect of the book potential readers see, it advertises the possibility for females to adopt a male 'heroic' guise, while also reinforcing the stigma that this type of behaviour in women is wrong.

While women turn to male narratives and male language for terms of self-expression that society would understand and accept, they are not confined to those terms. There is, in fact, an exclusively female hero archetype lurking among the brash males and terrifying the living daylight out of them. It is the witch. As Molly Brown justly notes, either demonised or sexualised, the witch is a source of both fear and yearning for members of the patriarchal community (2016). Fear, because she is an indispensable member of the community by virtue of fulfilling the tasks that men have declared taboo or suspect: midwifery, female health and emotional support are the key ones. Yearning, because she commands a power that no one can wrest from her, lest they be seen replacing her in all those unsavoury tasks listed above. The warrior princess contests with male characters on their own battlefield, that has been staked by generations of both real and fictional men; while the witch acknowledges the male province as being separate from her own area of influence. Characters like Galadriel, Polgera from *The Belgariad* (Eddings, 2004) or Lamia from *Stardust* do not bear arms, but I doubt any reader would hazard what it would be like to order them around. The witch is classless and raceless; or rather, she transcends social strata and ethnic boundaries, yet finds particular reflections in each of them. The witch takes otherness, a characteristic too long rubbed in women's faces, and makes it her own; she does not attempt to change herself in order to integrate with the male narrative, because she can and does exist independently. While the warrior-princess is defined, and limited, by her armour (that is, by her imitation of male heroes), the witch's connection to nature suggests an organic freedom and openness. An excellent example of this is Angela Slatter's *Of Sorrow and Such* (2015): a tale of Mistress Gideon raising an adopted daughter while also coping with the loss of her own mother in a world that persecutes witches and polices women. Slatter's expert description of human callousness is at times more violent than depictions of the bloodiest battles, and the struggle of the protagonist to preserve her own kindness in a society built on animosity strikes closer to home than tales of impossible feats of bravery. In the end, it is Mistress Gideon's refusal to be ashamed of who she is that carries her through the ordeal. Shame of ourselves and our imperfections in the face of the ideal society enforces on women is the main factor holding us back from embracing female characters who are not 'as strong as men', but who exist in and of their own right. The overarching question of the present essay collection is: do *we*, as readers, as writers, and as individuals, have a problem with female character representation in fantasy fiction? The issue lies not in the characters, but in our attitudes to them: the interpretation of male-coded heroines as largely positive and of characters in traditionally female roles as largely negative. Although it has been argued that language is a tool of oppression, it is better seen as a tool of coercion. By subscribing to male-heroic narratives, women describe themselves in a language of their oppression. They become complicit with the patriarchy that presents heroism, strength and tenacity as male virtues. Perhaps the problem is that we do not give enough credit to our heroines. They do not need to imitate men or to chase after the unattainable ideal of womanly perfection in order to represent us; they wear armour of a different kind.

Bibliography

Hahn, T. ed., 1995. The Wedding of Sir Gawain and Dame Ragnelle. In: *Sir Gawain: Eleven Romances and Tales.* Kalamazoo, Michigan: Medieval Institute Publications.

Foster, E.E. ed., 2007. Amis and Amiloun. In: *Amis and Amiloun, Robert of Cisyle and Sir Amadace.* Kalamazoo, Michigan: Medieval Institute Publications.

Hudson, H. ed., 2006. Sir Eglamour of Artois. In: *Four Middle English Romances: Sir Isumbras, Octavian, Sir Eglamour of Artois, Sir Tryamour.* Kalamazoo, Michigan: Medieval Institute Publications.

Baker, L-J., 2013. *Promises, Promises*. Maple Shade, New Jersey: Lethe Press.

Bardugo, L., 2012-2014. *The Grisha Trilogy: Shadow and Bone.* New York: Henry Holt and Co.

Brooks, P., 1992. *Reading for the Plot: design and intention in narrative.* Harvard: Harvard University Press.

Brown, M., 2016. Aching for Tiffany: Terry Pratchett's (Re)Visionary Witches. Presentation at the *International Medieval Congress.* Leeds, UK, 4-7 July.

Clare, C., 2010-2013. *Infernal Devices Trilogy*. New York: Margaret K. McElderry Books.

Eddings, D., 2004. *The Belgariad: Pawn of Prophecy*. London: Del Rey.

Friday, N., 1973. *My Secret Garden: Women's Sexual Fantasies*. London: Quartet Books.

Gaiman, N., 2001. *American Gods*. New York: HarperCollins.

Hounsom, L., 2015-2017. *The Worldmaker Trilogy: Starborn*. New York: Tor.

Jackson, R., 1981. *Fantasy, the Literature of Subversion.* London: Methuen.

Lewis, C.S., 1998. *The Chronicles of Narnia: The Lion, the Witch and the*

Wardrobe. London: Oberon.

McDougal, S., 2013. *I hate Strong Female Characters*. [online] 15 August. Available at: < http://www.newstatesman.com/culture/2013/08/i-hate-strong-female-characters> [Accessed 01 January 2017].

McRobbie, L.R., 2013. *Princesses Behaving Badly: Real Stories from History Without the Fairy-Tale Endings*. Philadelphia: Quirk Books.

Modleski, T., 2007. *Loving with a Vengeance: Mass Produced Fantasies for Women*. Abingdon: Routledge.

Negra, D., 2009. *What a Girl Wants? Fantasising the Reclamation of Self in Postfeminism*. Abingdon: Routledge.

Porath, Jason, 2017. *Rejected Princesses*. [online]. Available at: < http://www.rejectedprincesses.com> [Accessed 01 January 2017].

Russ, J., 1994. *The Female Man*. Toronto: Women's Press.

Russ, J., 1995. *To Write Like a Woman*. Bloomington: Indiana University Press.

Salzman-Webb, M., 1971. Woman as Secretary, Sexpot, Spender, Sow, Civic Actor, Sickie. In: M. Hoffnung Garskof, ed.,1971. *Roles Women Play: Readings Toward Women's Liberation*. Belmont, CA: Brooks/Cole. Pp. 7-24.

Scribbler, Ozzie, 2017. *Bikini Armor Battle Damage*. [online]. Available at: <http://bikiniarmorbattledamage.tumblr.com> [Accessed 01 January 2017].

Slatter, A., 2015. *Of Sorrow and Such*. New York: Tor.

Tolkien, J.R.R., 2007. *The Lord of the Rings*. New York: Harper Collins.

The Lord of the Rings: The Return of the King, 2003. [film] Directed by Peter Jackson. New Zealand: New Line Cinema.

Younger, B., 2003. Pleasure, Pain, and the Power of Being Thin: Female Sexuality in Young Adult Literature. NWSA Journal, 15(2), p. 45.

Wendel, S. and Tan, C., 2009. *Beyond Heaving Bosoms: the smart bitches' guide to romance novels*. New York: Simon and Schuster.

Gender-identity and sexuality in current sub-genres of British fantasy literature: do we have a problem?

By A J Dalton

The article considers why authors of fantasy, in trying to introduce more diverse representation into their work or to break away from the conventions of the genre, find themselves variously accused of racism, homophobia, misogyny and cultural appropriation. The article identifies how the 'epic fantasy' of the 1980s and 1990s was implicitly 'white and patriarchal', and how that sub-genre did so much to define and dominate the genre. Subsequent, inheriting sub-genres of fantasy - 'urban fantasy', 'dark fantasy', 'metaphysical fantasy' and 'grimdark fantasy', to name but a few - have had to work through, within and around the framework of the 'white and patriarchal' fantasy narrative in order to discover their own voices and representation. However, the article provides evidence that these later sub-genres have only succeeded up to a certain point.

A problem?

In a recent interview, the successful fantasy author Leigh Bardugo wonders why her first novel, *Shadow and Bone* (2012), is 'a very straight, very white fantasy', especially given that her 'peer group has never been particularly straight or particularly white' (Pippin, 2016). The explanation Leigh gives is 'I think I was writing to a lot of the fantasy that I had read […] it was my first foray, and it was only as I continued in that series that I found my voice and started building worlds that looked a little bit more like mine and the way I wanted the world to look.' It seems that the straight, white fantasy Leigh had grown up reading had created a framework that she had to work through and around, until she had subverted it enough that there was space and a place for her own voice. Is it, then, the task of the modern fantasy author to subvert the dominant gender-, identity- and sexuality-formulations of the fantasy literature that precedes them, if they are to express their own voice and assert their own 'self' and values? If so, the modern fantasy author does not start with a blank page, which surely represents a number of problems. Is a reader now required to be familiar with what came before in order to appreciate the subversion that the author is attempting? If the reader cannot 'appreciate' that subversion (perhaps they have not read the types of work that are being subverted or perhaps the subtlety of the subversion escapes them), is there a risk that they will begin to see the author as engaging in lazy stereotyping, tokenism, cultural appropriation or, worse, racism, misogyny and homophobia? Certainly such accusations have been levelled at even the likes of Scott Lynch[1].

Considering the above, the 'problem' for authors and readers of fantasy seems two-fold. First, because fantasy is genre fiction, there are particular – limiting and limited – motifs, character-types, social relationships and plot-

---

1. In an interview with Marcus Gipps at FantasyCon in Scarborough, UK, Sept 2016, Lynch described how the inclusion of a black character in one of his recent novels elicited 'a great deal of praise, but significant amounts of accusation around tokenism, cultural appropriation and racism'.

shapes that must be included (to a greater or lesser extent) if the work is even to be recognised as fantasy. Second, it would seem these 'requirements' of the genre embody and enact particular social and moral values to which the author or reader may well not ascribe, values which risk alienating both authors and readers alike. As societal values and priorities change, the dominant fantasy sub-genres of the past become out-dated or less immediately relevant to current readers. Those sub-genres of the past cannot simply be ignored, however, because they have greatly served to define the requirements of the genre[2]. Instead, current authors must reorganise, play with and subvert those past sub-genres in order to create the new and relevant sub-genre. To exemplify and better understand this creative challenge, negotiation and process, this article will describe just how the 'white' and 'straight' fantasy of the past finally gave way to such modern sub-genres as 'dark fantasy', 'metaphysical fantasy', 'dystopian YA' and 'grimdark fantasy'.

White and straight fantasy

The dominant sub-genre of fantasy literature in the UK during the 1980s and 1990s was 'epic fantasy'[3]. This sub-genre tended to take a working-class hero ('The Magician's Apprentice') as the protagonist, as in David Eddings's *Pawn of Prophecy* (1982) or Raymond E. Feist's *Magician* (1982), and send them on a 'Chosen One' (Kormack, 2015)

---

2. As argued in more detail in A J Dalton's article *George RR Martin and Tolkien have a lot to answer for*.

3. Although as early as 1977 Stephen Donaldson's Lord Foul's Bane had 'An Epic Fantasy' on the cover, effectively as a sub-title.

quest to save the world. Through hard work and moral virtue, they invariably succeed and are rewarded with a rise in social status and privilege (often through marriage), becoming a close friend and advisor to the royal family or a member of the magical elite. Implicit to this plot line, those at the top of society are described as morally enlightened, socially responsible and facilitators of social justice. Of course, such a plot line also echoed: a) the then Prime Minister Margaret Thatcher's personal and political story of starting out as a grocer's daughter, fighting to become a success and finally triumphing to become leader; and b) the Reaganomics version of the American Dream. 'Epic fantasy', therefore, provided the dramatic narrative that enshrined the traditional[4], conservative values of both the UK and US. These values described an improved quality of life as the reward for hard work and an acceptance of the status quo, thereby working to ensure that political power within these societies remained with white elites and those invested in a heteronormative patriarchy.

Perhaps unsurprisingly, the US and UK 'epic fantasy' of the 1980s was dominated in terms of international sales by white, straight, male writers like Donaldson, Feist and Eddings, all of whom wrote extended series in which the lead protagonist was male, straight and white. Although these authors arguably wrote 'strong' supporting female characters (such as Polgara and Ce'Nedra), those characters worked in service to the quest being led by the male protagonist, and just as frequently these authors wrote 'incidental' female characters to advance the plot and progress of the male

---

4. In an interview in Headway Upper-Intermediate, Margaret Thatcher describes those values as 'Victorian'.

lead. In Feist's *Magician*, for example, Pug rises to power through saving Princess Carline from mountain trolls, and in Donaldson's *Lord Foul's Bane* (1977) Thomas Covenant rapes a teenage girl who must then go on to guide him on his journey. Then, when a female character does not support the male quest and ambition, they are 'monstrous' (often sexually so) and to be defeated. For example, in Eddings's *Queen of Sorcery* (1982), the queen in question (Salmissra) is a seductive, malign and snakelike[5] being looking to waylay and possess the young male lead (Garion).

Such authors continued to be successful into the 1990s, and new ones arrived, including Terry Goodkind (*Wizard's First Rule*, 1994) and L. E. Modesitt Jr (*The Saga of Recluce*, beginning 1991), but this decade also saw a significant increase in the number of female authors of this sub-genre being published or seeing improved sales. By way of example, in the UK there were J. V. Jones (*The Baker's Boy*, 1995), Maggie Furey (*The Artefacts of Power*, beginning 1994) and Juliet E. McKenna (*The Thief's Gamble*, 1999), to name the most prominent, and in the US there were the likes of Robin Hobb (*Assassin's Apprentice*, 1995), Mercedes Lackey (numerous contemporaneous series), Marion Zimmer Bradley (numerous contemporaneous series) and Sheri S. Tepper (numerous contemporaneous series). It was such female authors who began to provide female leads, but it is of note that these authors tended to be more commercially successful with series featuring male leads, series which conformed to the patriarchal heteronormativity even as they attempted to address themes

---

5. All but a combination of Eve and the serpent in the book of Genesis.

of marginalisation and change.

The popularity and dominance of 'epic fantasy' only increased during the 1990s[6], but it was probably the sub-genre's unusual longevity and degree of dominance that contributed to its eventual decline, for fantasy had become extremely 'formulaic'[7], if not entrenched, to the extent that it did not or could not adjust so easily to changes in society in order to remain relevant to readers. There was a sense that society and the genre were in denial or retrograde, and that there was a difficult moment of self-realisation coming. The millennium was coming. We were faced with Y2K and a new dark age for humanity. It was in such a context that the backward-looking sub-genres of 'steampunk'[8] and 'flintlock fantasy'[9] emerged, along with the more subversive sub-genres of 'urban fantasy'[10] and the 'comedic fantasy' of

---

6. There was a proliferation of titles and authors, as detailed in A J Dalton's *The Sub-genres of British Fantasy Literature*.

7. The term 'formulaic' is often used by readers of the genre I speak to (at my book signing events), publishing professionals and fantasy authors to describe the 'epic fantasy' of the 1990s, as seen on such websites as www.vision.ae and The Caffeinated Symposium.

8. The term 'steam-punks' was coined by K. Jeter in a letter to Locus magazine in 1987 (http://www.jessesword.com/sf/view/327), but the term was not used in a book title until Paul Di Filippo's 1995 Steampunk Trilogy.

9. The term 'flintlock fantasy' was coined by the reviewer Andrew Darlington in reference to Stephen Hunt's *For the Crown and the Dragon* (1994), as described in an interview with Hunt, by De Joode, on The Book Plank website.

10. The sub-genre of 'urban fantasy' grounded fantasy and its readers, in that it was deliberately first-world, set in a familiar urban landscape, and offered a certain grittiness along with its fantastical or supernatural elements. More often than not, the plots revolve around some sort of serious crime (murder, kidnapping, assassination, etc.) or insidious threat

Sir Terry Pratchett.

Millennial fantasies

The proliferation and competition of 'steampunk', 'flintlock fantasy', 'comedic fantasy' and 'urban fantasy', with the arrival of the new millennium, marked the end of the numerous decades in which a single sub-genre dominated, represented or defined the genre, its social moment and its wider society. The fractures, class divides and competing groups and voices within society were becoming more obvious. Social certainties were replaced by social anxieties, and competing values now informed social and individual identity. The early 2000s thereby foreshadowed and predicted the greater crisis of 2008/09 onwards, the time of the credit crunch and the time during which UK politicians were found guilty en masse of the Expenses Scandal, the tabloid press were culpable in the Phone Hacking Scandal, and the police were found guilty of the Selling Information Scandal. It was clear to all that we were not ruled and safeguarded by those of superior moral standing, of a noble conscience and with a sense of social responsibility. No longer could the frameworks of 'high fantasy'[11] and 'epic fantasy' be offered as valid. Even 'steampunk', 'flintlock

---

(a shadowy mafia or creeping sort of corruption) that threatens not just the protagonist but also the wider society. A classic example of the genre is Neil Gaiman's *Neverwhere*, which was first aired as a BBC radio show in 1996 and released as a novel later the same year.

11. The works of Tolkien are often used to define 'high fantasy' (Stableford, 2005), a sub-genre written with gravitas and an almost religious sense of good and evil, whereas 'epic fantasy' witnesses more humour and variety amongst its characters.

fantasy', 'comedic fantasy' and 'urban fantasy', the fantasy sub-genres of the early 2000s, were quickly to be supplanted by the 'dark fantasy', 'dystopian YA', 'metaphysical fantasy'[12] and 'grimdark fantasy' of the late 2000s onwards.

Into darkness

With the approaching credit crunch and the onset of the various corruption scandals previously mentioned, the first-world 'urban fantasy' of the early 2000s evolved into first-world 'dark fantasy'. Both sub-genres concern themselves with modern romantic relationships but, where 'urban fantasy' tends to observe patriarchal heterosexual norms (the good guy 'wins' the girl), 'dark fantasy' is more morally ambivalent, there are no out-and-out good guys and sexual congress is considered 'dangerous' and often to be resisted i.e. everything is 'darker'. So, for example, where Joss Whedon's *Buffy the Vampire Slayer* (1997-2004) sees Buffy falling for (and making traditional, unthreatening love with) male vampires who invariably possess or seek a human soul, by contrast the lead female role of Bella in the *Twilight* (Meyer, 2005-08), played in the movie version by the gay Kristen Stewart, actively seeks a sexual relationship with Edward that is likely to destroy her. She is repeatedly reminded of the dangers of sexual consummation and is almost killed by a subsequent pregnancy and childbirth

---

12. More morally ambivalent and existential than 'epic fantasy', the sub-genre of 'metaphysical fantasy' was first coined in Jan 2008 with the release of A J Dalton's *Necromancer's Gambit*, a novel badged with 'The best of Metaphysical Fantasy'; the sub-genre is now a category of fantasy literature on Amazon.

ordeal, an ordeal that is described in truly horrific terms. Then, in *True Blood* (late 2008-2014), we are presented with a far wider range of dark alternative relationships and lifestyles, from the abstinent, to S&M, to the pansexual, to the sinful, to the grotesque, to the fatal, to the drug-fuelled, to master-slave, to the orgiastic. Thus, the development from 'urban fantasy' to 'dark fantasy' represented mainstream society's anxiety concerning – and its getting to grips with – the true diversity of orientations, preferences and identities. With the elites and the establishment revealed as corrupt and morally redundant, the traditional heroes and values of society were abandoned and there was a turning to, representation of and 'acceptance' of other and more diverse voices in society (voices that had traditionally been marginalised, represented as socially undesirable or as belonging to 'the dark side').

Where 'epic fantasy' (particularly of the 1980s), with its second-world whimsy, noble kings, beautiful queens and heroic males, was supplanted by 'urban fantasy' (of the early 2000s), with its first-world grit, street life and battling females empowered by several male lovers, 'urban fantasy' was in turn supplanted by 'dark fantasy' (of the late 2000s), with its diversity of lifestyle, sexuality, personal definition and representation. The groups that were previously hidden, demonised, marginalised or condemned by society (be they Goth, Emo, LGBTQ, androgyne, dysmorphs, multi-racial, non-identifying or other) were at last given open and explicit representation. Indeed, for its time, and as a mainstream TV series, *True Blood* was particularly explicit in terms of its portrayal of sex, violence and difference.

Yet 'dark fantasy', as progressive and welcomed as it

was initially, also caused furious debate amongst both fans and critics and suffered something of a backlash. Just as much as *True Blood* received praise for depicting the black, gay character of Lafayette, the series was accused of tokenism, racism (Sarah, 2011), homophobia and cultural appropriation[13] (Rod, 2010). Just as much as the series was praised for its open and explicit representation, it was accused of being voyeuristic, gratuitous (MadameAce, 2014) and demeaning to the lifestyles represented. Just as much as the series was praised for presenting an empowered female lead, the series was accused of the patriarchal and misogynistic use of women as sex objects (Tapson, 2014). Just as much as the series was praised for its stand on civil rights ('vampire rights'), it was accused of being 'muddled' (Peitzman, 2013) on rights issues. Just as much as 'dark fantasy' was progressive compared to 'urban fantasy' and 'epic fantasy', it was soon considered by certain sections of a rapidly changing society to be too white, patriarchal, whimsical and exploitative.

Where white female authors were exploring via 'dark fantasy' what it was to be female in a post-2000 society, white male authors like A J Dalton (*Necromancer's Gambit*, 2008, *Empire of the Saviours*, 2011), R. Scott Bakker (*The Darkness That Comes Before*, 2004) and Alan Campbell (*Scar Night*, 2006) were exploring via 'metaphysical fantasy' what it was to be a white male now that the traditional male heroes and social values of 'epic fantasy' were exposed as being very much at odds with the sociohistorical moment, impossible for readers to identify with, redundant and

---

13. In terms of both the content of the series and the issue of the writer, Charlaine Harris, being white and straight.

the controlling narrative and political ideology of the old regimes. In the same way that first world 'dark fantasy' represented the transition of first-world 'urban fantasy' to a more modern sociohistorical context, so second-world 'metaphysical fantasy' represented the transition of second-world 'epic fantasy' to a more modern consideration. Just as 'dark fantasy' brought darker themes, understanding and outlooks to 'urban fantasy', so 'metaphysical fantasy' did the same for 'epic fantasy'.

Both 'metaphysical fantasy' and 'epic fantasy' concern themselves with the 'Chosen One' quest to save the world from evil forces but, where 'epic fantasy' tends to see the pre-existing social and moral order triumphantly restored (with the protagonist rewarded via social advancement), 'metaphysical fantasy' is more morally ambivalent in terms of the narrative outcome, there are no out-and-out winners (indeed, mere survival often comes at a hefty price) and social advancement is never quite the prize it is promised to be, i.e. everything is darker. So, for example, where the 'epic fantasy' novels of Raymond E. Feist's *Magician*, David Eddings's *Pawn of Prophecy* and J. V. Jones's *The Baker's Boy* all see a good-hearted boy (the 'Chosen One') from the kitchens become friends with royalty while undertaking a quest that saves the world, reaffirms key social values and ennobles society, the 'metaphysical fantasy' novels of my own *Necromancer's Gambit* and *Empire of the Saviours* see a socially marginalised individual as Chosen One go on a quest that defeats the enemy but also shatters society in the process[14]. Where 'epic fantasy' ends with glorious triumph

---

14. Titles including Alan Campbell's *Scar Night* (2006) and R. Scott Bakker's *The Darkness That Comes Before* (2004) also fit this general

and celebration, the 'triumph' at the end of 'metaphysical fantasy' is pyrrhic at best, all but genocidal or apocalyptic at worst. Where 'epic fantasy' self-congratulates and throws itself a party or feast, 'metaphysical fantasy' sees the protagonist left to bury the dead, grieve over loved ones and try to pick up the pieces of a broken world. Where 'epic fantasy' is about what can be won, 'metaphysical fantasy' is about what has been lost. Implicitly, then, where 'epic fantasy' endorses the society and values that determine success, 'metaphysical fantasy' explores, questions and even challenges them. Thus, the development from 'epic fantasy' to 'metaphysical fantasy', coinciding with the elites and establishment revealed as morally corrupt and redundant, represented society's increasing anxiety and discomfort concerning its traditional values, shamed heroes and so-called role models, as well as its treatment of socially marginalised groups; the development saw epic and ennobled heroes and social values abandoned in favour of those who had previously suffered heroically as marginalised individuals or groups.

Inevitably, the 'heroic' masculinity and male sexuality represented in 'metaphysical fantasy' are very different from the patriarchal hetero-normativity of 'epic fantasy'. In 'metaphysical fantasy', the sexually aggressive male of 'epic fantasy' is dead, literally in the case of *Necromancer's Gambit*, is sublimated into a spiritual will, as with *Scar Night*'s angelic lead or *The Darkness That Comes Before*'s messianic antagonist, is a marginalised anachronism, as with the Scourge in *Necromancer's Gambit* and Cnaiür

---

plot shape, so the label 'metaphysical fantasy' might retrospectively be applied to them.

urs Skiötha in *The Darkness That Comes Before*, or is the rapine and duplicitous enemy. All these books contain sexually abstinent monks, hermit-like magicians, morally ambivalent male characters and cowardly male characters who are nonetheless successful. Although male combat is presented (even more graphically than in 'epic fantasy'), it often resolves little; with equal frequency positive outcomes are achieved through verbal argument, negotiation and declaration. Combat is only decisive when there is no option left and the fundamentally opposing ideologies of the parties involved force 'the final battle'. Even then, as mentioned before, that final confrontation does not bring the sort of glory and male affirmation that is described in 'epic fantasy'. Instead, we are left with a sense of grief, anxiety concerning the future and helplessness. We are left with questions and doubts concerning the potency/impotence of male will and desire.

Perhaps unsurprisingly, just like 'dark fantasy', 'metaphysical fantasy' quickly received as much praise as it did negative criticism. As much as the sub-genre was considered 'fresh' and 'different' (Gipps, 2008) the male lead was often considered to be too 'wimpy'[15] and the fight scenes were described as being overly declarative or too symbolic. The plot progression was considered 'too intellectual', self-indulgent, reflective and 'talking-based'[16].

---

15. https://www.amazon.co.uk/Empire-Saviours-Chronicles-Cosmic-Warlord/dp/0575123133/ref=sr_1_1?ie=UTF8&qid=1479378009&sr=8-1&keywords=empire+of+the+saviours.
16. https://www.amazon.co.uk/product-reviews/1841494089/ref=cm_cr_dp_hist_one?ie=UTF8&filterByStar=one_star&reviewerType=all_reviews&showViewpoints=0.

Finally, the outcomes were seen as too 'dour' or 'gloomy'[17]. Just as much as 'metaphysical fantasy' was progressive compared to 'epic fantasy', it was soon considered by certain sections of a rapidly changing society not to celebrate the white male or patriarchy sufficiently.

It seems that what had been lost with 'epic fantasy' was a consensus on, or acceptance of, what was right and wrong, what values should be supported, what was socially desirable and undesirable, what was acceptable and unacceptable behaviour, what were acceptable and unacceptable beliefs, what defined gender and sexuality, and what it was to be a responsible person in modern society. With the loss of the moral and social certainty represented within 'epic fantasy', 'dark fantasy' and 'metaphysical fantasy' could only offer confused or angst-ridden protagonists. Indeed, the protagonists of both first-world 'dark fantasy' and second-world 'metaphysical fantasy' struggle for a sense of identity and existential meaning. Given that this 'crisis' of identity in the mid-to-late-2000s sits in stark contrast to the sense of moral and social certainty, superiority and security found pre-9/11 (2001), the move from 'epic fantasy' and 'urban fantasy' to 'dark fantasy' and 'metaphysical fantasy' can be understood as a corollary to the emergence and development of the 'Millennial'[18] self: an individual

---

17. https://www.amazon.co.uk/product-reviews/033044476X/ref=cm_cr_dp_hist_two?ie=UTF8&filterByStar=two_star&reviewerType=all_reviews&showViewpoints=0.

18. The term was first coined by William Strauss and Neil Howe in 1987, and more fully described in their 1991 book Generations: *The History of America's Future*, which was followed in 2000 by *Millennials Rising: The Next Generation*.

reaching young adulthood around the year 2000, sometimes known as 'Generation Y'. Where the generation preceding[19] the Millennial self could simply share in and espouse the traditional values of their parents and society (the 'epic fantasy' sub-genre was unusually dominant for the two decades before 2000), the Millennial self experienced a break or disconnect from (what had been) social reality. This disconnect is more often than not represented in 'dark fantasy' and 'metaphysical fantasy' as protagonists being exiled, abandoned, cast adrift or suffering the surreal experience of being the dead/undead in the world of the living. *Twilight* begins with Bella being taken to the airport in sunny Phoenix and boarding a plane to 'a small town named Forks [which] exists under a near-constant cover of clouds' in order to live with her estranged father. *Empire of the Saviours* sees Jillan exiled from Godsend and separated from his parents in the first chapter. And *Necromancer's Gambit* opens with Saltar being raised from the dead against his will, both with little memory of who he previously was when alive and with an inability to trust the controlling necromancer who has fundamentally sinned in raising him. What these three examples also have in common, of course, is a disconnect with authority figures and wise counsellors, those who pass on the traditional values of society, promote conformity and ensure the individual's experience of the world is manageable and ultimately benign. Indeed, where Bella's parents are largely absent in *Twilight*, the kings and rulers in *Empire of the Saviours* and *Necromancer's Gambit* are conspicuously corrupt, insidious and malign.

---

19. 'Generation X'.

The plot progression of 'dark fantasy' and 'metaphysical fantasy' therefore involves the protagonist's fraught quest to discover a sense of identity and self, to find a place in the world, and to find safety and contentment. Invariably, however, these two sub-genres ultimately describe terrible sacrifice, loss, anti-climax and resignation. The self-realisation, place, safety and contentment that are achieved are illusory or temporary at best. There is no true 'happy ending', as the existential quest of life continues on through the next generation(s), some progress made but the results of past mistakes born into the future, the problems of society and the past inherited by those that follow on after us. In *The Twilight Saga*, the final battle which destroys both the protagonist Cullens and antagonist Volturi is anti-climactically revealed to be a mere foretelling, one which actually dissuades the Volturi from starting the battle at all (or postpones it to a more distant future), leaving Edward and Bella with their rapidly maturing hybrid daughter to their lives in the 'perfect peace' of their small cottage, lives that are surreal, sublimated and heavenly precisely because they cannot actually exist in the real world: 'And then we continued blissfully into this small but perfect piece of our forever' (Meyer, 2008:768). In my *Flesh & Bone Trilogy*, the final scene has Mordius and Saltar discussing the essentially different and disruptive nature and inheritance of Saltar's son Orastes, how the people must eventually lose their faith in the gods, that the balance will fail, and that 'the damage is already done and that one day this realm must end' (Dalton, 2010:362). Finally, my *Chronicles of a Cosmic Warlord* end with a pregnant Hella asking Jillan if their child will be safe and her realising that 'If they're anything like their father, they'll still find ways to get into trouble' (Dalton, 2014:365)… and then the Epilogue presents us with the antagonist Declension successful once more in another realm ('He would see the Declension claim the cosmos for itself', 368), with the Peculiar looking on: 'Still, wouldn't things be boring if they became too easy?' (369).

'Dark fantasy' and 'metaphysical fantasy', then, do not ultimately provide 'solutions' to all the societal problems with which they contend. Although there are confrontation and accountability described, the problems are ultimately shared by all and continue into the future. In the UK, that future (the early 2010s) saw all of society apparently sharing in the pain of the credit crunch and austerity, but it soon became apparent that the pain was not being shared equally, that the rich were only becoming comparatively richer, that failed executives (arguably those responsible for the crash) were still receiving massive bonuses, and that it was the less privileged classes who were truly paying for the mistakes and greed of the privileged classes. (Neither should we forget the previously mentioned MPs' expenses scandal, the phone hacking scandal and the police selling of information scandal that were also ongoing.) The resentment, anger and disillusionment resulting from these revelations inevitably saw the 'dark fantasy' and 'metaphysical fantasy' of the late 2000s replaced with the 'dystopian YA' and 'grimdark fantasy' of the early 2010s.

Even darker

Both near-future, first-world 'dystopian YA' and second-world 'grimdark fantasy' describe an immoral or lawless society in which those at the top are the most corrupt, immoral or bullying. There are themes of abuse, betrayal and abandonment present throughout both sub-genres. Both sub-genres describe a loss of innocence and the gaining of a hard-won cynicism.

In the 'dystopian YA' novels of *The Hunger Games Trilogy* (Collins, 2008-10), the *Escape from Furnace* series (Smith, 2009-11), the *Divergent* trilogy (Roth, 2011-16) and the *Maze Runner* series (Dashner, 2009-16), we are presented with death-match game shows featuring youth, the unjust imprisonment of youth, the institutionalised murder of youth, surgical experimentation on youth, and the use of youth as military fodder. The lead protagonists (both male and female) usually lose their family, have 'friends' based only on sharing the predicament of other youths and do not have anyone they can trust enough to form a successful romantic relationship. Very much, we are presented with admirable but lonely protagonists. Their sense of self, gender-formation and sexuality are oppressed to the extent that they are elided or prevented from developing. The true 'self' can only be realised by breaking free of the society that forces them to conform. There is a sense of constant monitoring and scrutiny, a need to hide the 'self' so that it might be protected from exploitation, and a creeping paranoia. So, although 'dystopian YA' represents a more gender-balanced set of protagonists, protagonists whose sexuality remains private and unjudged by others, there is a constant wariness about expressing a clear gender-identity and sexuality, and certainly no celebration of distinct gender-formations and sexual difference.

Similarly, in the second-world 'grimdark fantasy' novels of *A Song of Ice and Fire* (Martin, 1996-2016), *The Demon Cycle* series (Brett, 2008-16), *The Broken Empire Trilogy* (Lawrence, 2011-13) and *The First Law* series (Abercrombie, 2006-16), we are routinely presented with torture, rape, brutalisation, the flaying of skin and mass slaughter (usually perpetrated by males). The sub-genre describes such horror unflinchingly, with a numb matter-of-factness or with a shocking sense of detachment; although there is much that is gratuitous in such work, the literature is satirically post-traumatic, defiantly desensitised and utterly disillusioned. Indeed, the horror is so extreme but mundane that a profound sense of nihilism, mental exhaustion and an apocalyptic desire for self-destruction plagues all. So, although in ways 'grimdark fantasy' liberates the heroic white male from the oppressive social control of 'epic fantasy', and all gender-formations and sexualities experience 'equal' treatment, the results for these heroes (most of whom die), their families (most of which are raped and murdered) and their societies (most of which perpetrate the sort of mass-scale slaughter that threatens the survival of humankind) are self-defeating. The white, patriarchal, heroic males of 'epic fantasy' are thereby portrayed as being just as culpable as the society that formed them. It is therefore interesting that this literature is particularly written by white, heterosexual, male authors of the patriarchal societies of the UK and US. These are self-aware and self-reflective authors, just as their protagonists have extremely cynical and ironical voices.

Yet hope is not entirely absent (particularly in 'dystopian YA'), for the existential quest of the defiant protagonist still drives the narrative of both sub-genres. 'Dystopian YA' tends to culminate in the youthful protagonist successfully escaping or destroying the institutions of the corrupt society, and even 'grimdark fantasy' offers us an anti-hero to introduce a new social order (albeit that the anti-hero often fails in their long-term aim). We might finally wonder how best to summarise the 'solution' offered by these two sub-genres. Some might describe it as 'civil war', some as anarchy and terrorism. Some might welcome such a solution, some might see it as inevitable and others still would advocate fighting to resist it. Perhaps that is another story, one for those with 2020 vision.

Progress?

Conservative 'epic fantasy' and 'urban fantasy' moved into 'metaphysical fantasy' and 'dark fantasy', which moved into 'grimdark fantasy' and 'dystopian YA'. Can things get even darker? The UK and US have seen Brexit and the election of a right-wing Trump government. European populations have elected more right-wing governments. There is more intolerance of difference and more insistence upon traditional values… but also more resistance and more protest than before. We are seeing subversion, assertion and reversion. Societies are more polarised and fraught than ever before.

This year (2016), a number of UK and US fantasy conventions have had panel debates on 'epic fantasy', a number of mainstream publishers (HarperVoyager included) have had open submissions requesting 'epic fantasy' novels and I have had fans emailing me asking why there isn't more 'epic fantasy' around (Dalton, 2016).

It seems that some people yearn for a return to that 'golden age' of fantasy. They want to see hope restored. Yet they are calling for a sub-genre which offers hope only to a certain few, a sub-genre which works to ensure that political power within society remains with the traditional white elites and those invested in a hetero-normative patriarchy.

It would seem that Leigh Bardugo, a majority of fantasy authors and fantasy readers are going to have their problem for a little while yet. The problems of fantasy literature are the problems of the world. To quote Bardugo herself from the interview mentioned at the start:

I also think one of the reasons people try to shut YA down so often, why they turn their nose up at it, is because it's absolutely terrifying to them when women and girls begin to dictate the culture and make their minds up for themselves.

Bibliography

Abercrombie, J. 2006-16. *The First Law* series. London: Gollancz.

Bakker, R.S., 2004. *The Darkness That Comes Before*. New York: Overlook Press.

Bardugo, L., 2012. *The Grisha Trilogy: Shadow and Bone*. New York: Henry Holt and Co.

Brett, P.V., 2008-17. *The Demon Cycle* series. London: HarperCollins.

Buffy the Vampire Slayer, 1997-2003. [TV programme] Directed by Joss Whedon. Fox.

Campbell, A., 2006. *Scar Night*. New York: Tor.

Collins, S., 2008-10. *The Hunger Games Trilogy*. New York: Scholastic.

De Joode, J., 2014. *Author interview with Stephen Hunt*. [online] Available at: <http://thebookplank.blogspot.co.uk/search?q=Darlington> [Accessed on 01 July 2016].

Dalton, A.J., 2008. *Necromancer's Gambit*. Bloomington: AuthorHouse.

Dalton, A.J., 2010. *Necromancer's Fall*. Bloomington: AuthorHouse.

Dalton, A.J., 2012. *Empire of the Saviours*. London: Gollancz.

Dalton, A.J., 2013. *George RR Martin and Tolkien have a lot to answer for*. [online] Available at: < https://www.scifinow.co.uk/blog/fantasy-author-a-j-dalton-asks-why-do-we-all-sound-like-george-rr-martin> [Accessed 18 March 2013].

Dalton, A.J., 2014. *Tithe of the Saviours*. London: Gollancz.

Dalton, A.J., 2016. *New trends in fantasy and scifi*. [online] Available at: < https://metaphysicalfantasy.wordpress.com/2016/11/05/new-trends-in-fantasy-and-scifi> [Accessed on 5 November 2016].

Dalton, A.J., 2017. *The Sub-genres of British Fantasy Literature*. Edinburgh: Luna Press Publishing.

Dashner, J., 2009-16. *Maze Runner* series. New York: Delacorte Press.

Donaldson, S.R., 1977. *Lord Foul's Bane*. New York: Holt, Rinehart and Winston.

Eddings, D., 1982. *Pawn of Prophecy*. London: Del Rey.

Eddings, D., 1982. *Queen of Sorcery*. London: Del Rey.

Feist, R.E., 1982. *Magician*. New York: DoubleDay.

Furey, M., 1994. *The Artefacts of Power*. New York: Spectra.

Gaiman, N., 1996. *Neverwhere*. London: BBC Books.

Gipps, M., 2008. *Exchange between Marcus Gipps, commissioning editor at Gollancz, and A J Dalton*. [email] (Personal communication, August 2008).

Goodkind, T., 1994. *Wizard's First Rule*. New York: Tor Fantasy.

Hobb, R., 1995. *Assassin's Apprentice*. New York: Voyager Books.

Hunt, S., 1994. *For the Crown and the Dragon.* s.l.: Green Nebula Publishing.

Jones, V., 1995. *The Baker's Boy*. New York: Aspect.

Kormack, M., 2015. *In Defence of the Chosen One*. [online] Available at: < http://fantasy-faction.com/2015/in-defence-of-the-chosen-one> [Accessed 11 July 2016].

Lawrence. M., 2011-13. *The Broken Empire Trilogy*. London: HarperCollins.

MadamAce, 2014. *True Blood Season 3: Tara, Misogyny, and Rape Culture*. [online] Available at: < https://ladygeekgirl.wordpress.com/2014/12/04/true-blood-season-3-tara-misogyny-and-rape-culture> [Accessed on 4 December 2014].

Martin, J.R.R., 1996-2016. *A Song of Ice and Fire* series. London: HarperCollins.

McKenna, J.E., 1999. *The Thief's Gamble*. New York: Harper Voyager.

Meyer, S., 2005. *Twilight*. New York: Little, Brown and Company.

Meyer, S., 2006. *New Moon*. New York: Little, Brown and Company.

Meyer, S., 2007. *Eclipse*. New York: Little, Brown and Company.

Meyer, S., 2008. *Breaking dawn*. New York: Little, Brown and Company.

Modesitt Jr, L.E., 1991. *The Saga of Recluce*. New York: Tor Forge.

Peitzman, L., 2013. *Why the Civil Rights Allegory on True Blood is so Misguided.* [online] Available at: < https://www.buzzfeed.com/louispeitzman/why-the-civil-rights-allegory-on-true-blood-is-so-misguided?utm_term=.ojbOa4A18#.xpwx8ZBVy> [Accessed on 25 June 2013].

Pippin, C., 2016. *In Conversation with Rainbow Rowell and Leigh Bardugo.* [online] Available at: <https://www.buzzfeed.com/chelseypippin/worlds-collide?utm_term=.dod9yrXpG#.pqMoY7RWy> [Accessed 15 December 2016].

Rod, 2010. *True Blood's Charlaine Harris on Gay Rights and Bisexual Vampires.* [online] Available at: < http://rodonline.typepad.com/rodonline/2010/05/true-bloods-charlaine-harris-on-bisexuality-and-gay-vampires.html> [Accessed on 01 May 2010].

Roth, V., 2011-16. *Divergent* trilogy. New York: Katherine Tegen Books

Sarah, 2011. *Racism in True Blood.* [online] Available at: < http://ftvms2102011.blogspot.co.uk/2011/08/racism-in-true-blood.html> [Accessed on 25 August 2011].

Smith, A.G., 2009-11. *Escape from Furnace series*. London: Faber & Faber.

Stableford, B., 2005. *The A to Z of Fantasy Literature*. Plymouth: Scarecrow Press.

Strauss, W. and Howe, N., 1991. *Generations: The History of America's Future*. New York: William Morrow.

Strauss, W. and Howe, N., 2000. *Millennials Rising: The Next Generation*. New York: Vintage Books.

Tapson, M., 2014. True Blood' and Misogyny. [online] Available at: < https://acculturated.com/true-blood-and-misogyny> [Accessed on 30 July 2014].

True Blood, 2008-2014. [TV programme] US: HBO.

Tipping the Fantastic: How the Transgender Tipping Point Has Influenced Speculative Fiction

By Cheryl Morgan

Fantasy, and more particularly science fiction, has always been interested in changes of gender. For most readers it seems to be a remarkable, if not magical, thing. For trans people, however, it is a fact of life. It hasn't escaped our notice that most fiction about us is written very much from the point of view of people fascinated by our apparent transformations. With trans people becoming more visible in the media, and Time magazine proclaiming a "Trans Tipping Point", has speculative fiction kept pace with society, and if so how is it different now?

In May 2014 Time magazine put Laverne Cox on the cover and proclaimed a Transgender Tipping Point. Since then the mainstream media has developed an obsession with trans people, for both good and ill, but how has speculative fiction dealt with this? Do we have a trans problem?

At first glance, science fiction at least has always been interested in trans people. The very idea of medically changing sex (and let's elide over what being trans means for now) has a science-fictional feel to it. The *Encyclopaedia of Science Fiction* dates stories about gender transformation at least as far back as 1924 (SFE, 2017). Fantasy has an even older tradition of magical transformations, including Ovid's *Metamorphoses* (approx. 8 CE, read in 1986 translation). However, the vast majority of such stories have been told by people who are not trans (cis people[1]). While they may have a (sometimes prurient) interest in trans people, their understanding has often been lacking.

A particular issue is the obsession with the process of transition. Cis people are understandably fascinated by the fact that people's gender can change, but the result of this is that trans people are seen as interesting only because of their transition, not as people in their own right. It is a process of objectification. This seems to be particularly true in YA literature, presumably because publishers feel the need to address issues that they believe to be facing young people, and do so in an educational and informative way. However, if that is what they are doing, they seem to be doing it with a curious (and perhaps voyeuristic) cis audience in mind.

The problem in YA is more obvious in mimetic fiction, a prime example being the much-lauded[2] *Luna* (2004) by Julie Peters. The story is told from the point of view of the trans character's cis sibling, and mostly focuses on how hard it can be to have a trans person in the family. The story's "happy ending" is that the trans character leaves home forever.

Another problem is that cis people writing about trans characters often have little understanding as to why people might transition. In science fiction, for example in Iain

---

1. The word "cis" is now commonly used to mean "not trans" on the basis that cis and trans are Latin prefixes meaning "on this side" and "on the far side". The prefix, trans, is used in many English words to mean to cross to the other side or to travel to some far place. A cisgender person is thus someone who has stayed with the gender they were assigned at birth, while a transgender person has moved away from that gender.

2. It was a finalist for a National Book Award (USA) and Lambda Literary Award (LGBT books), among many other honours.

M. Banks Culture series (most prominently in *Excession* (1996)) or Alastair Reynolds' *Chasm City* (2001), gender transition is seen primarily as a possible life choice that long-lived characters might make, rather than something that people need to do in order to live honest and authentic lives. This portrays being trans as a "choice", which inevitably suggests that it is a choice that need not be made, or which can be forbidden by law.

Alternatively transition may be shown as a route to social privilege or power. This is very explicit in Lois McMaster Bujold's *A Civil Campaign* (1999), where a woman transitions to male in order to inherit a title in a patrilineal society. Less obviously, in Lila Bowen's *Wake of Vultures* (2016), a character is described as trans because she crossdresses in order to get a job as a cowboy, but never shows any great affinity for masculinity. Such stories feed the myth that trans men are simply trying to move up the social scale and gain male privilege, and suggest that claiming to be trans is a cover for some more nefarious purpose.

Nevertheless, speculative fiction has been on a journey. Inclusion and representation of trans characters has improved over time. Before we look at better examples, however, it would be wise to set out what we mean by a character being trans.

For many people the idea of a trans person still equates to what is known as the "classic transsexual"; that is someone born with a body that fully conforms to one of the two poles of the gender spectrum, who has an intense need to live as a person of the other extreme of gender, and seeks medical aid to transform their body to enable this. While such people do exist (and I am a fairly typical example), modern understanding of trans people encompasses a much wider classification identities.

We should first note that the idea that the human race (or any other species of animal for that matter) exists only in one of two possible genders is biological nonsense. Many people are born with biological characteristics that, in the two-gender model, are a mixture of male and female. There are animal species in which this is more common; where more than two genders exist; and where transition between genders is a natural part of the animal's lifecycle. Humans with such intersex conditions may identify as trans, or may not, in part because they may be very happy with the gender they were assigned at birth and have no wish to change it.

In addition we now accept that full medical transition is inappropriate for many trans people (and unaffordable for many more). Large numbers of people identify as "non-binary" in some way, meaning that neither extreme of gender suits them. Such people may opt for partial medical transition or none at all. Non-binary people can include those who see themselves as belonging to a third gender, as flipping between the two gender extremes, or as rejecting the idea of gender altogether.

A further complication is that the way in which people understand their gender is related to the culture in which they live. There are people who live outside of the binary gender system in all cultures, but the way in which a Western person might understand a trans identity can be quite foreign to a hijra in India[3], a two-spirit[4] person from one of the native

---

3. Even within India, hijra may see their identity differently depending on whether they are Muslim or Hindu.

4. Two-spirit is a modern umbrella term used to encompass a wide

peoples of North America, or to a Polynesian islander[5].

The vast majority of portrayals of trans people in speculative fiction have conformed in some way to the Western model, primarily because Western culture dominates the field, even in many cases where the author has a different cultural history. Nevertheless, other examples can be found if you look for them.

The journey that speculative fiction has been on is perhaps exemplified by Ian McDonald. In 1996 he published *Sacrifice of Fools*, which, through an analogy of someone who wants to become an alien, suggests that trans people are sad fools who can never truly become the object of their obsessions. It was not one of McDonald's finest moments, though the book did have a lot of good things to say about the unhappy situation in Northern Ireland. The book was shortlisted for the Tiptree for its exploration of gender, which shows how little understanding of trans issues Tiptree juries sometimes have.

However, by 2004 McDonald's message had changed significantly. *River of Gods* features a character called Tal who identifies as a "nute", an agender[6] person. Tal's character arc is a transition story. McDonald does a good job of describing the social ostracism faced by trans people, and the complexity of the medical transition process. He also creates a culture for the nute community, including

---

variety of Native traditions. Each individual Native people had its own understating of gender.

5. Each island group in Polynesia has its own words for trans people.

6. That is, a person without gender. Tal undergoes complex surgery to remove all gender markers from the body while still allowing sexual arousal.

adoption of a non-binary pronoun. "Yt" might not have been the best choice of pronoun, but at least the issue was acknowledged and addressed.

In *Brasyl* (2007) McDonald has moved on again. The central character, Edson, is bisexual and gender fluid[7]. Neither of these identities is key to his character arc. They are just aspects of who he is. In *Luna: New Moon* (2015) many of the younger characters are non-binary in some way. That's just how Lunar society is. Gender, for them, is mutable and flexible. The sequel, *Luna: Wolf Moon* (2017), continues the story and one character notes, "We live in the most gender-fluid society in human history." (Location 3366 of a Kindle Advance Reading Copy).

McDonald, then, provides an excellent example of a writer who is aware of the changing attitudes towards trans people in the real world, and who uses those attitudes as part of his worldbuilding for near-future societies. Other writers have tried to look deeper at the social and political consequences.

An excellent recent example is the *Jacob's Ladder* trilogy[8] from Elizabeth Bear. At first sight it is a simple generation ship story, albeit one with a highly gender variant crew. However, in the third book, *Grail* (2011), we learn why the crew left Earth in the first place. They belong to a faction of humanity that wants to use medical technology for personal fulfilment, including gender transition if necessary. In contrast, the government on Earth wants to use medical technology to force people to fit into stereotyped views of

---

7. He regularly presents in a very feminine manner in addition to his more usual masculine presentation.

8. *Dust* (2007), *Chill* (2010) and *Grail* (2011).

gender by "curing", or eliminating, anyone whose gender or sexuality is deemed socially undesirable. It is a very pertinent question, and one that we will doubtless find more pressing in the real world as research into the biological underpinnings of sexuality and gender progresses.

Two authors, Melissa Scott and Kim Stanley Robinson, have addressed the issue of how a future society might change to become more accepting of a variety of genders. In *Shadow Man* (1995) Scott speculates that the physical demands on the human body exacted by interstellar travel lead to a medical treatment that, as a side effect, significantly increases the number of intersex births. The world of the book exhibits five distinct human genders, an idea derived from a famous essay, "The Five Sexes: Why male and female are not enough" (1993), by the biologist and gender studies professor, Anne Fausto-Sterling. The book is set on an isolated and deeply conservative world where the local culture refuses to accept this aspect of reality and tries to force everyone to conform to the old binary gender model. The book is, of course, in part a satire about modern day America.

Robinson's book, *2312* (2012) postulates the discovery that people with a particular intersex condition live significantly longer than people whose bodies are purely male or purely female. The result of this is that people now have their children modified in utero to have the desirable intersex characteristic. The idea that having intersex children could be a fashion started by the super-rich is rather amusing, but Robinson fails to follow through on the gender issue because his two main characters (in what is essentially a romance) are fairly stereotypical in their performance of masculinity and femininity.

On a more philosophical level, science fiction has often been used to ask what it means to be a woman. Typically this has been done by using androids of some sort. In his Gideon Smith series David Barnett does this via Maria, a steampunk automaton. In *Gideon Smith & The Mask of the Ripper* (2015) Maria meets Gloria, a trans woman, and they sit in a coffee shop having a conversation about what being a woman means to them. This is something that can't really be done outside of speculative fiction.

While these philosophical explorations by the likes of Bear and Barnett can be fascinating, and indeed are a core part of science fiction's mission, they still objectify trans people to some extent because the purpose of the trans character(s) being in the book is to examine some facet of gender. McDonald has shown, in *Brasyl* and *Luna: New Moon*, that a character, even a central character like Edson, can be trans without that being in any way important to the plot of the book. Being trans is simply who that person is, and is no more significant to the plot than a choice of ethnicity, hobbies or eye colour. From a trans activism point of view, this sort of inclusion is much preferable because it acts to usualise[9] rather than exoticise the trans characters.

There are now many examples of authors who have chosen to include trans characters simply as part of the background of the world. In *The Galaxy Game* (2014) Karen Lord has a supporting character who is non-binary. N.K. Jemisin's Hugo-winning *The Fifth Season* (2015) includes a

---

9. The word "usualise" has been adopted by LGBT+ campaigners because "normalise" would suggest that LGBT+ people are in some way abnormal.

trans woman as a supporting character who, because of her parentage, may become very significant in the final volume of the trilogy. And Emma Newman's *After Atlas* (2016) has a non-binary character who is a well-known investigative journalist. In all of these cases, the fact of the character being trans is neither germane to the plot, nor a matter of any great concern to the other characters.

Fantasy authors too have stepped up to the plate and included trans characters in their books. Sometimes this happens in a modern-day urban fantasy setting, such as Paul Cornell's *Who Killed Sherlock Holmes* (2016). Sometimes magic is used in a fantasy world to effect a transformation, for example in Glenda Larke's Watergivers Trilogy (specifically in *Stormlord Rising* (2010)). And sometimes trans characters manage the best they can, as they did in our world before medical transition methods were invented. Examples of this are *Eon* (2008) and *Eona* (2011) by Alison Goodman, *Karen Memory* (2015) by Elizabeth Bear and *The Black Opera* (2012) by Mary Gentle.

One potential banana skin for the fantasy writer, however, is to assume highly advanced magic but little or no magical help for gender transition. In a world where life-threatening wounds can be healed quickly and easily, how likely is it that no one managed to develop any spells to help with gender transition? Larke gets this right, explaining how healing magic was used to change her trans character's body. Failure to consider this possibility is one of the (many) limitations of *The Bone Palace* (2010) by Amanda Downing.

Fantasy can also be used to explore gender issues. One fascinating example of this is Rachel Hartman's *Shadow*

Scale (2015). In this book, the central characters visit a city in which the local culture recognises six genders. One of these is the gender normally used for strangers[10]. As one of the locals explains, it is impolite to assume a gender for someone. You should use the stranger gender for any new person that you meet until such time as you have been able to ask, "how may I pronoun you?"

Because fantasy is often set in the past, it can be used to illustrate trans history. Stephanie Burgis' *Masks and Shadows* (2016) is set in Austria in the late 18th Century. The book is a romance, but the male half of the couple is actually a castrato singer, Carlo Morelli. Carlo probably would still identify as male, but not all castrati did. Perhaps more importantly, Burgis takes aim at the concept that all eunuchs were fat and ugly. Castrati were the rock stars of their day. They needed to be elegant and cultured to please their aristocratic patrons and were apparently in great demand as lovers as well as singers[11].

Fantasy can also be used to illustrate the cruelty experienced by trans children. Seanan McGuire's *Every Heart a Doorway* (2016) is set in a school for young girls who have been kidnapped by fantasy worlds and then spat back out into the mundanee world. Mostly these young women are simply pining for the life they once knew as princesses in a land of wonders, but one pupil, Kade, is a trans boy.

---

10. And also for gods and aubergines.
11. The term "castration" can mean many different types of medical procedure, ranging from full removal of the genitals to a simple vasectomy. Some methods of making a eunuch could leave the patient sexually potent, if not fertile.

Kade was still living as a girl when kidnapped, but in his fantasy world he was able to grow into himself, eventually becoming a Goblin Prince. The fantasy world spat him out because it no longer recognised him as a girl. As is the way of such things, he returned home the same age as when he left and found himself once again faced with the threat of female puberty. This time it is his parents who reject him, dismissing his male identity as a mere fantasy. Interestingly, Kade is one of the more mature and sensible pupils, because all that matters to him is to be able to be himself, regardless of which world he happens to be in.

Every Heart a Doorway is also notable for the fact that the main protagonist, Nancy, is asexual.

A particular issue faced by authors is how to reveal the fact that a character is trans. If done awkwardly, this can prejudice the reader against the character and make it appear as if some sort of deception is being practised. The most famous example of the "shock reveal" is in Neil Jordan's film, *The Crying Game* (1992)[12]. One of the best examples of a no-fuss reveal I have seen is in *The Root* (2016) by Na'amen Gobert Tilahun. Two male characters are engaged in a friendly fighting bout as part of their physical training. The following exchange takes place:

> *All of a sudden Erik was free. He groped for his balance, fell, and his palm slammed into Tae's hip. The other boy hissed but it quickly cut off.*
> *"You okay?"*
> *"Yeah, just my injection site, I thought it wouldn't*

---

[12]. In which discovering that a woman you fancy is trans is very literally sickening.

> *hurt since it's all healed up, but it's still sensitive."*
> *"Injection site?"*
> *"Testosterone."*
> *"Oh, got it." Erik smiled and nodded. (218)*

That's all that was necessary. Tae being trans isn't mentioned again in the book because at no point does it become relevant.

Very occasionally authors may get drawn into questions of trans politics. This may be some of the cause behind the treatment of the trans woman in Amanda Downing's *The Bone Palace*. This character is initially set up as being very feminine, but is progressively revealed to be more of a man in drag. A more serious example is Mary Gentle's *Ilario* duology[13]. On the one hand, this is a superb book about the problems faced by an intersex person in a mediaeval world. However, it also includes a character who identifies as a trans woman but is shown to be "really a gay man" by the story. The contrast between the valid (biological) condition of the intersex character and the presented-as-fake identity of the trans woman is very marked.

While trans people make up a fairly small proportion of the human population, we are not so rare as to be absent from the author community. Indeed, being an author is exactly the sort of solitary, non-customer-facing occupation that is open to a group of people who are regularly discriminated against in the employment market. Trans writers have, of course, always been with us, but in the past they were less able to be out, and therefore less willing to write about trans

---

13. The Lion's Eye (2006) and The Stone Golem (2007).

issues. Rachel Pollack was one of the pioneers, winning the Arthur C. Clarke Award with *Unquenchable Fire* in 1989 and famously introducing the trans superhero, Coagula, in DC's *Doom Patrol* comic in 1993.

With a greater social acceptance of trans people, more of us have been able to get published, and to write freely about issues that affect us. The most high profile of the current crop of trans writers is Caitlín R. Kiernan who won Best Novel at the World Fantasy Awards with *The Drowning Girl* (2012). While the trans character in the book, Abalyn, is not hugely prominent, she is very sharply and painfully observed.

Roz Kaveney is a good example of someone who, despite a glittering career as a critic and journalist, was unable to get fiction published until the current explosion of interest in trans issues. Her ongoing fantasy series, *The Rhapsody of Blood*[14], has an extensive cast of queer characters. The major trans character in the series is such an outrageous authorial choice that I'm not going to risk spoilers by discussing it here. Suffice it to say that I think it works very well.

Short fiction is perhaps an easier way for trans people to get published as so much of it comes from small presses that are free of the corporate anxieties of larger organisations. Brit Mandelo's *Beyond Binary* (2012) explores a wide range of different sexualities and genders. Lethe Press, which has been publishing anthologies of year's best gay and lesbian speculative fiction for some time, has recently added *Transcedent* (2016), a series edited by K.M. Szpara, which will showcase the best trans-themed and trans-authored

---

14. *Rituals* (2012), *Reflections* (2013) and *Resurrections* (2014) thus far.

short fiction of the year. *The Janus Cycle* (2015) by Tej Turner has each chapter told by a character of a different sexuality and/or gender. Topside Press, which specialises in work by trans authors, is in the process of producing an anthology of science fiction and fantasy written and edited by trans writers. They had over 250 submissions[15].

One of the most interesting anthologies featuring trans writers is *Love Beyond Body, Space, and Time* (2016), edited by Hope Nicholson. All of the authors identify as LGBT+ in some way, but in addition they all identify as Native American. This gives us a very different take on trans identities to that provided by writers coming from Western cultures.

While it is heartening that so many trans writers are getting their work published, it is noticeable that almost all of it comes through small presses. Of the above-mentioned works, only *The Drowning Girl* is from a mainstream publishing house. Charlie Jane Anders has been signed by a big publisher, but her only novel to date, *All the Birds in the Sky* (2016), doesn't have any significant trans characters. This suggests that there may be some reluctance among mainstream speculative fiction publishers to tackle trans themes.

An area of mainstream publishing that trans writers are starting to move into now is YA fiction. As noted above, most of the YA featuring trans characters is realistic, and tends towards attempts to explain trans people to a cis audience. Trans characters in YA speculative fiction are rare, but two recent books are beginning to change things

---

15. Email from the editors, Casey Plett & Cat Fitzpatrick, 18th February 2016.

on this front.

When the Moon Was Ours (2016) is a delightfully lyrical novel by Anna-Marie McLemore. It is the sort of thing that is likely to get classified as magic realism rather than speculative fiction, and not just because of McLemore's Hispanic background. The book features two trans characters, one of whom has been the beneficiary of a magical transformation and one who is still an adolescent who has only transitioned socially. McLemore clearly understands the issues faced by trans people well, which is hardly surprising as she is married to a trans man. This, together with the sheer quality of the writing, make this book one that is likely to be a go-to text on trans issues for some time.

The other YA book I want to mention is *Dreadnought* (2017) by April Daniels. This also features a trans person who benefits from a magical transformation. However, in her case a side-effect of the transformation is that she has also become Earth's mightiest superhero. Daniels uses this setting to highlight many of the social disadvantages facing trans people. For example, the hero's parents, unaware that she welcomes the transformation, start investigating gender reassignment techniques in the hope of getting their "son" back; something they would have rejected outright had she needed it to transition to female. The book is very funny, and a nicely crafted superhero novel. I hope it does well.

The final book I want to mention is *Full Fathom Five* (2014) by Max Gladstone. It is one of the very few books listed here where the trans character is the central viewpoint character of the novel. Kai is many years post-transition when the events of the novel occur, and she has benefitted from a magical transformation so she has none of the social issues faced by real-world trans people. On the surface it looks like there is no reason for her to be trans at all. And yet, there she is.

Presumably Gladstone had some reason for making Kai trans. Perhaps it was simply matter of diversity, and no more important than the decision to make her female, or non-white. If that's so, it is quite remarkable enough. However, reflecting on the book after I had finished reading it, it occurred to me that Gladstone may have done something more. Kai's job, at a corporation that deals in spirituality and faith, requires a great deal of self-confidence and strength of will. These are things that trans people need in abundance growing up in a world that constantly requires them to deny who they are and pretend to be someone else.

What we may have, in *Full Fathom Five*, is a book where the author has not just decided to have a hero who is trans, but where he has created a hero whose trans nature is an active advantage to her in the work she does, and in overcoming the challenges she faces during the novel. If that's so, and Gladstone has said nothing on the issue himself, then we have something quite remarkable.

What can we conclude from all of this? Does speculative fiction have a trans problem? Hopefully in the above I have made it clear that things have improved, and are continuing to improve. Things are, I think, much better than they were 20 years ago. That doesn't mean that there isn't room for improvement.

As I noted above, most of the speculative fiction featuring trans characters, and almost all of the speculative fiction by trans writers, comes from small presses rather than from mainstream publishers. While anyone who is aware of the variety and quality of small presses in the speculative fiction community can access these books, they will be invisible to anyone not deeply embedded in that community. It doesn't help that publicity materials for books, and reviews will often ignore the trans element in the book. This was even the case for *Brasyl*, where the lead character is flamboyantly bisexual and gender fluid.

On several occasions I have seen young people on social media bemoaning the lack of specific trans content in speculative fiction. I know this is wrong, but I can quite understand why readers come to such a conclusion. In any case, of the above books, only *Brasyl*, *Dreadnought* and *Full Fathom Five* have a trans character as the main protagonist.

Had I written this essay a year ago I would have said that trans characters are almost completely absent from YA speculative fiction. Thankfully that has changed, but it is too early to say whether the change will stick.

Something else that is notable is that, of all the trans authors mentioned above, only K.M. Szpara identifies as a trans man, and he's listed here as an editor (though he does have a number of professional short fiction sales). In addition, the majority of trans characters mentioned are trans women. While it is easy for anyone reliant on mainstream media for their knowledge of trans people to assume that the vast majority of trans people are trans women, this is not true. In fact recent surveys suggest that by far the largest group is people who identify as non-binary[16]. If it is important

---

16. Official US and UK government estimates of the size of the trans population are 0.6% and 1% respectively, but the studies these numbers

that trans characters are included to reflect the diversity of humankind, then surely we must reflect the full variety of trans people, including a multiplicity of ethnicities, not just one subgroup.

I could, of course, mention Billy Martin at this point. However, he pretty much ceased to write following his transition and he announced his retirement in 2010 (Martin, 2010).

There is, therefore, quite a way to go. However, I have some confidence that things will continue to improve. In particular, I am keeping a close eye on three YA authors: Juno Dawson, Fox Benwell and Elliot Wake. All three had successful careers before transitioning, so have no choice but to be out. Their proven track records should make it easier for them to write what they want. None of them are specifically speculative fiction writers, but as young people today have grown up in a world saturated with popular media that uses speculative fiction themes, it would not surprise me to see any of them produce non-realist books.

---

were based on did not look at non-binary people. Recent surveys in The Netherlands and New Zealand which did include non-binary people suggest a trans population in excess of 4%.

Bibliography

Anders, C.J., 2016. All the Birds in the Sky. New York: Tor.

Banks, I.M., 1996. Excession. London: Orbit.

Barnett, D.M., 2015. *Gideon Smith and the Mask of the Ripper*. London: Snowbooks.

Bear, E., 2007. *Dust*. New York: Spectra.

Bear, E., 2010. *Chill*. New York: Spectra.

Bear, E., 2011. *Grail*. New York: Spectra.

Bear, E., 2015. *Karen Memory*. New York: Tor.

Bowen, L., 2016. *Wake of Vultures*. London: Orbit.

Bujold McMaster, L., 1999. *A Civil Campaign*. Wake Forest, NC: Baen Book.

Burgis, S., 2016. *Masks and Shadows*. New York: Pyr.

Cornell, P., 2016. *Who Killed Sherlock Holmes*. London: Pan Macmillan.

Daniels, A., 2017. *Dreadnought*. New York: Diversion Publishing.

Downing, A., 2010. *The Bone Palace*. London: Orbit.

Fausto-Sterling, A., 1993. The Five Sexes: Why male and female are not enough. The Sciences, March/April 1993:20–24.

Gentle, M., 2006. *Ilario: The Lion's Eye*. London: Gollancz.

Gentle, M., 2007. *The Stone Golem*. London: Gollancz.

Gentle, M., 2012. *The Black Opera*. San Francisco: Night Shade Books.

Gladstone, M., 2014. *Full Fathom Five*. New York: Tor.

Goodman, A., 2008. *Eon*. New York: Viking.

Goodman, A., 2011. *Eona*. New York: Viking.

Hartman, R., 2015. *Shadow Scale*. New York: Random House.

Jemisin, NK., 2015. *The Fifth Season*. London: Orbit.

The Crying Game, 1992. [film] Directed by Neil Jordan. UK: Palace Pictures & Channel Four Films.

Kaveney, R., 2012. *Rhapsody of Blood: Rituals*. San Francisco: Plus One Press.

Kaveney, R., 2013. *Rhapsody of Blood: Reflections*. San Francisco: Plus One Press.

Kaveney, R., 2014. *Rhapsody of Blood: Resurrections*. San Francisco: Plus One Press.

Kiernan, C.R., 2012. *The Drowning Girl*. New York: Roc.

Larke, G., 2010. *Stormlord Rising*. London: Orbit.

Lord, K., 2014. *The Galaxy Game*. London: Del Rey.

McDonald, I., 1996. *Sacrifice of Fools*. London: Gollancz.

McDonald, I., 2004. *River of Gods*. New York: Simon & Schuster.

McDonald, I., 2007. *Brasyl*. London: Gollancz.

McDonald, I., 2015. *Luna: New Moon*. London: Gollancz.

McDonald, I., 2017. *Luna: Wolf Moon*. London: Gollancz.

McGuire, S., 2016. *Every Heart a Doorway*. New York: Tor.

McLemore, A., 2016. *When the Moon Was Ours*. New York: Thomas Dunne.

Mandelo, B. ed., 2012. *Beyond Binary*. Maple Shade, NJ: Lethe Press.

Newman, E., 2016. *After Atlas*. New York: Roc.

Nicholson, H., 2016. *Love Beyond Body, Space, and Time*. Winnipeg, MB: Bedside Press.

Ovid, 8 AD. *Metamorphoses*. Translated from Latin by A.D. Melville.,

1986. Oxford: Oxford University Press.

Peters, J., 2004. *Luna*. New York: Little, Brown and Company.

Pollack, R., 1988. *Unquenchable Fire*. New York: Overlook Press.

Pollack, R., 1993-1995. *Doom Patrol,* 64, 87. New York: Vertigo.

Reynolds, A., 2001. *Chasm City*. London: Gollancz.

Robinson, K.S., 2012. *2312*. London: Orbit.

Scott, M., 1995. *Shadow Man*. New York: Tor.

Szpara, KM., 2016. *Transcendent*. Maple Shade, NJ: Lethe Press.

Tilahun, N.G., 2016. *The Root*. San Francisco: Night Shade Books.

Turner, T., 2015. *The Janus Cycle*. s.l.: Elsewhen Press.

SFE, 2017. *Transgender SF*. [online] Available at: <http://www.sf-encyclopedia.com/entry/transgender_sf> [Accessed 17 February 2017].

Martin, B., 2010. *I'm Basically Retired (For Now)*. [online] Available at: <http://docbrite.livejournal.com/2010/06/09> [Accessed 14 February 2017].

Badass Bisexual Babes: Shameless Titillation or Empowered Characters Embracing Their True Selves and Sexuality?

By Hazel Butler

The twenty-first century is increasingly accepting of the full spectrum of gender identities, sexuality, and sexual preference. We see an increasing number of characters in Fantasy who embrace different aspects of this spectrum. Their validity as representations of the LGBTQS community can be brought into question, however, by characters whose sexual expression is less a reflection of true diversity, and more an attempt to titillate audiences with same-sex action while keeping main characters 'straight at heart' to preserve the mainstream appeal of central romantic relationships. This study will examine a number of notable examples of bisexual characters in Fantasy and consider whether their gender identities and sexuality, as portrayed, are a genuine reflection of a more diverse approach to characterisation, or a cheap trick to boost ratings and gain publicity.

Introduction

Literary icon and socio-political activist Rita Mae Brow once said, 'We're all degrees of bisexual'. Sexuality, much like gender, does not exist in a binary state. Although modern Western culture is deeply rooted in strict binary notions of 'male' and 'female', 'straight' and 'gay', the desire to neatly package people into one of two easily understood options goes against human nature.

To be bisexual is, simply put, to acknowledge you are

attracted to both sexes. Whether you act upon those feelings is an entirely different matter. Attraction does not always equate to action. As society becomes more accepting of the concept of bisexuality, people are feeling increasingly comfortable describing themselves as existing somewhere along the spectrum between absolute 'heterosexual' and absolute 'homosexual'.

Strangely it is this mid-point on the spectrum that is proving difficult for modern society to embrace and fully comprehend. We are so set in our binary, black and white view of the world, that it's very difficult to believe individuals exist who, for want of a better expression, love all people equally.

Misconceptions and Misrepresentations

While mainstream popular culture is increasingly accepting and representative of the LGBTQ community, bisexuality is one letter in the acronym that is frequently left out, or misrepresented. In the bid to be fully representative of gay and lesbian characters, bisexual characters are few and far between. Those characters who do engage in relationships with both sexes are almost always portrayed as being gay, or straight, with an exception or two. Characters identify as gay, lesbian, transgender, and transsexual, but very rarely as *bisexual*.

Those who are, frequently fail to represent the very real characters and characteristics of the bisexual community, but often portray stereotypes, caricatures, and only help to reinforce misconceptions about bisexual individuals.

Bisexuality is a spectrum within the spectrum. There is

no neat divide down the bisexual heart dictating they love women and men equally. Some bisexuals are attracted to both equally, yet some prefer one gender or the other, while some are *drawn* to both, but only enter into relationships with one.

Biphobia and Bierasure

Bisexual characters face two very real, and extremely frustrating issues, in the form of biphobia (the fear of bisexuality), and bierasure (the erasure of a person's bisexual nature, once they settle into a committed relationship). The former manifests in much the same way as homophobia or racism, however it is not limited to the straight community. There are many in the LGBTQ community who are frustrated by characters who appear to be gay but appear to be heteronormalised into a straight relationship when they ultimately choose a character of the opposite sex. This feeds into bierasure, which essentially negates a person's bisexual nature and assumes that, once they are in a relationship, they are now either straight or gay, depending upon their ultimate choice of partner.

As if the bisexual nature is simply an inability to choose, and bisexuals are fickle creatures who can't truly be defined until they've made that decision and settled down.

The choice of partner erases their status as a bisexual, either in the eyes of the author or audience. Past relationships are no longer of consequence, and the fact they are in a committed relationship means they are no longer attracted to people of a different gender to their partner.

The reality of the bisexual nature is very different. Those

who identify as bisexual remain queer regardless of who they are with, or what kind of relationship they are in. They remain bisexual, much as they remain male or female, white or black.

Bisexuality is not a choice that can be made and unmade. It is an intrinsic part of a person's identity. The only questions are whether or not one accepts it, and whether or not one chooses to act on all their desires.

Common Problems...

Before delving into some specific portrayals of bisexuality in Fantasy, it is helpful to outline some of the common problems that crop up across the genre.

Side-lining
Bisexual characters experience 'best friend syndrome' as much as any other minority group in fiction. We're all familiar with the tropes: gay best friend, black best friend, Asian best friend... When it comes to quirky, and indeed queer, the world seems reasonably content to accept bisexual characters as the oddball best friend/minor character. From barely present siblings, to mysterious absentee love interests, to the ex that left the main character crushed, bisexuality exists on the fringes of Fantasy more often than not.

Characters of a bisexual nature seldom get to be the stars of the show, whether that show is on the page, the silver screen, or in syndication.

The B-Bomb
Some books shy away from profanities, others embrace

them, yet more find a happy medium. But the F-Bomb isn't nearly as explosive in this context as the 'B-Bomb'. A great many characters who openly embrace sexual and emotional relationships with both genders, and in many ways appear to be extremely open-minded, simultaneously avoid, and sometimes even stigmatise, the word 'bisexual'.

This appears to be due to the belief that this is more inclusive: labelling bisexuality diminishes it or misrepresents it. But by avoiding the word, any headway made in raising awareness and understanding of bisexuality is confused by sending a very clear (if unintentional) message that there is something *wrong* with being bisexual.

Literally. The word itself is taboo. It should never be spoken.

Caricatures vs. Characters

While cardboard cut-out characters are in no way a new problem, there is a marked tendency to avoid fleshing out the characteristics and backstories of bisexual characters. While the motivations, histories and emotional reactions of straight and gay characters are often explored in detail, the bisexual occupies a murky realm in which cause, motive, thought, and feeling frequently fail to exist.

It's arguable that the lack of backstory is not because they're bisexual, but simply because they're bit parts. Due to the minor roles, it's likely that little backstory would be provided for these characters regardless of their orientation. The unfortunate effect of this is that a great many bisexuals in fiction are caricatures, rather than characters. This is compounded by the fact that many bisexuals in pivotal roles also lack depth. Their motives are unclear, their feelings aloof.

Our experiences, hopes, dreams, needs and wants shape our desires and decisions. To understand a character fully you need to know their motivation. The lack of exploration when it comes to many bisexual characters leads to them seeming shallow, not because bisexuality is shallow, but because there's no depth, motivation, or explanation for their feelings and actions.

Lost Voices

The result of these tendencies is that bisexual characters often lose their voices. It's rare to experience a story from the point of view of a bisexual. This, coupled with their tendency to play minor roles and lack of explanation for their actions and reactions, leaves bisexuals voiceless in fiction more often than not. Pivotal events take place in their lives, and the only context we have for the impact it has on them comes from the observations of others. Very rarely do we see what they see, feel how they feel. Instead, we have assumptions, perceptions and misconceptions given to us by other characters, most of whom have no point of reference for what this sexual minority is going through in terms of their sexuality because they are not bisexual.

The Good, The Bad, And The Ugly...

There are some good examples of bisexual characters who are handled well in Fantasy. Sarah J Maas' *Throne of Glass* series (Maas 2012-2016) features Aedion Ashryver, a main character who is openly bisexual, yet in the present time of the series interested in a woman. This fact does not negate his history or the fact he's had relationships with both men and women in the past. He's not seen (either by himself or other characters) as a straight guy with an 'experimental phase' he's left behind. He's bisexual. It just so happens his current love interest is female.

Another good example of bisexuality well-handled is Maggie Stiefvater's *The Raven Cycle* (Stiefvater 2012-2015), and the character of Adam Parrish. Adam has relationships with women but ultimately ends up in a relationship with a man. His relationship with his boyfriend does not negate his bisexuality in any way. He is not portrayed, or perceived by other characters, as gay. He's simply Adam.

Audrey Coulthurst (2016) portrays a similar situation in *Of Fire and Stars*, in which she depicts a relationship between two women. Of the pair, Denna identifies as gay, and is portrayed as such, Mare, on the other hand, is bisexual, despite being in a stable relationship with a woman.

The characters of Amira in *Otherbound*, by Corinne Duyvis (2014), Colton in Tara Sim's *Timekeeper* (2016), as well as the titular character in Laura Lam's *Michah Grey Series* (Lam 2013- 2015) are yet more examples of bisexual characters successfully depicted as engaging in committed relationships while retaining their bisexual identity. Jacqueline Carey's *Kushiel's Legacy Series* (2001-2011) depicts a world in which bisexuality is not only widely accepted, it's almost expected, with the added twist that religion condones and fully encourages the bisexual nature with a simple command: 'love as thou wilt'.

The trouble with the search for bisexuality in Fantasy is that you have to unhook your eyes a bit, turn your head and squint. Once you stop looking for the self-proclaimed, easily identified bisexual, you realise that bisexuality can be found in abundance throughout the Fantasy genre. It's often subtle, and it's not always well done, but bisexual characters *do* exist, and in higher numbers than one might imagine.

There are some great characters who openly admit to bisexuality, like Lorcan in Sarah Maas' *Empire of Storms* (2016), Magnus Bane in Cassandra Clare's *Shadowhunter Chronicles* (2007-2014), and Taema in Laura Lam's *False Hearts* (2016).

There are also a plethora of intriguing characters whose sexuality is entirely open to debate, like The Fool in Robin Hobb's *Realm of the Elderlings Series*. The character appears initially as an apparently male Fool, at the court of King Shrewd in *The Farseer Trilogy* (1995-1997), before featuring in *The Liveship Trader's Trilogy* as Amber, an apparently female mystic (1998- 2000). The gender and sexual orientation of the character are directly brought into question during *The Tawny Man Trilogy* (2001-2003), during which the character switches between his personas of the Fool and Amber, depending on the company he's in, and declines to answer any direct questioning on the matter. He expresses interest in characters of both sexes and doesn't appear to hold either in higher regard than the other. Ultimately the question of The Fool's gender and sexual orientation are irrelevant: The Fool loves Fitz. That this love is unrequited, and the object of his affections is so utterly incapable of accepting the truth of his/her nature, is part of the great tragedy of the character.

Other subtle examples of bisexuality come in the form of Tanya Huff's *The Fire's Stone* (2015), which features two bisexual male leads. Interestingly, the *Blood Books* (1991-

1997) by the same author feature a bisexual male vampire lead. Henry Fitzroy's bisexuality isn't a major plot point to the novels but it is expressed and evident throughout the series; an excellent example of bisexuality well handled. The TV adaptation, however, *Blood Ties*, made no reference to it whatsoever and portrayed the character as completely straight.

While a complete discussion of every instance of bisexuality in Fantasy would be impossible, there are a few examples that bear looking at in more detail...

True Blood

HBO's hit series *True Blood* (2008-2014) has arguably done more good for the LGBTQ community than any other Fantasy series in recent memory, awash as it is with characters of all manner of persuasions. Based on Charlaine Harris' *Southern Vampire Mysteries* (2001-2013), anyone who has read the books knows the series dug considerably deeper into the world Harris created. The characters are more varied, versatile, and far more three-dimensional. The TV show has never shied away from LGBTQ themes, yet it struggles with stereotyping. Lafayette is one of the most well rounded portrayals of a gay character in mainstream television, yet he's incredibly stereotypical in a lot of respects, as are Talbot and Steve Newlin, arguably the first character in the series who could genuinely have been portrayed as bisexual. Instead, he is a rampaging juggernaut of stereotypes: closeted gay man with a trophy wife; bigoted preacher; gay man forcing himself on straight man (played for laughs) and camper than rows of tents.

Tara could also have been an interesting bisexual character. For the first few series she bounces from one doomed crush to the next dysfunctional fling, and a deranged liaison with a psychopathic vampire, before running away to find herself and recover from the endless trauma inflicted on her by men. Tara's transformation is riddled with stereotypes. She falls for a woman and suddenly develops a love of kickboxing. Not only that, despite her frequent hook-ups with men in the past, she never looks at another man again. She had the potential to be a great bisexual character, but instead she moved seamlessly from 'unlucky in love straight girl' to 'adventurous/butch lesbian' without batting an eyelid.

The only truly decent portrayals of bisexual characters are James and Sophie-Ann. The latter is a vampire queen who regularly takes male and female lovers with no preference. Unfortunately, Sophie-Ann's appearances are few and far between.

James is quite different. The original actor who portrayed the character at the end of season six, Luke Grimes, quit the show because (according to HBO), he objected to 'the creative direction of the character' and refused to be involved in same-sex scenes (Hewett, 2014). Newcomer Nathan Parsons took on the role and did an excellent job of portraying a man torn between the woman he loves, who doesn't truly love him in return, and a man who offers him the kind of love, respect and understanding he craves. The fact that one is male and the other female doesn't faze him in the least, and he is not depicted as a man discovering he's gay, but rather a man who accepts his bisexual nature and has had relationships with both men and women in the past.

The disappointment, where James is concerned, is that he didn't show up until the final season.

The only other male character to demonstrate genuine bisexuality is Eric, one of Sookie's main love interests. While his seduction of Talbot is entirely motivated by revenge, he comments that it's 'been a while' since he slept with a man (Season 3, Episode 8, 'Night on the Sun'). He's so blasé about it and so comfortable in his sexuality that the effect is that of a man who has happily taken both male and female lovers over the course of his (long) life. That he prefers female companionship doesn't diminish this element of his character, and it casts a new light on his teasing interactions with Lafayette and some of the other male characters.

Sadly, however, the only true screen time given over to this side of Eric comes as he's killing Talbot, and during the numerous and blatantly gratuitous sequences in which straight male humans have vivid sexual dreams about male vampires (who have given them their blood in order to heal them). These scenes serve absolutely no purpose beyond titillating the audience. They are not there for character or plot development, and often act as bait-and-switch scenes to trick the audience into thinking one thing is happening, provide several minutes of shameless sex everyone knows full well isn't real, before cutting back to the male dreamer feeling shame and disgust at having had the dream. Not only that, the dream sequences frequently cut out before any explicit male-on-male acts have taken place.

Dreams of this nature are, by contrast, treated as an exciting bonus to a vampire encounter when they take place between straight characters. In particular, Sookie's many and varied dreams involving Bill and/or Eric.

The marked difference in the portrayal of sex scenes between straight, gay, and bisexual characters in the show is not limited to the dream sequences. The series openly embraces full nudity and extensive sex scenes between straight characters, yet the sexual encounters between the gay characters in the series are played down. Lafayette and Jesus are a particularly good example of this, appearing in dim lighting and usually with several layers of clothing, compared to the fully nude and very well-lit bodies of straight couples. Lesbian scenes in the series, on the other hand, are often exaggerated and played up for the benefit of the audience.

The message in all this seems to be clear: straight sex is good television, girl-on-girl action is great fun, and boys getting it on is fine, as long as it's not *really* happening, or takes place in the dark.

Lost Girl

Lost Girl (2010-2016) is one of the few instances in mainstream television that depicts a bisexual character as the lead on a show, rather than relegating them to the role of sidekick. Bo is a succubus, a female supernatural being who feeds on the life force of others through sexual contact. Initially she is portrayed as only feeding on the energy of evil individuals. She lacks control and doesn't wish to hurt anyone. As the series progresses, however, Bo discovers she's a Fae and learns control. Freed of her long-held belief that she is an evil creature, she embarks on a relationship with a male werewolf called Dyson. The relationship is complicated, however, by a second love interest in the form of Lauren, a human doctor.

The show is refreshingly original not only in its willingness to portray a bisexual character as the protagonist, but also to provide a love triangle in which the two parties vying for her affections are not the same sex. There is genuine chemistry between Bo and both Dyson and Lauren. The latter is a genuine budding relationship rather than a distraction thrown in for fun, or to titillate the audience. Bo is a well-rounded, fully developed character, whose interest in both men and women is treated as reasonably equal. We do not have the sense she is straight and experimenting, or that she is a lesbian now that she has forged a relationship with a woman.

On balance, the show does an extremely good job of portraying bisexuality. There is, however, a caveat. Throughout the series there is the sense that Dyson is Bo's soul mate, while Lauren is simply of interest to her while Dyson isn't around. The general impression given is that Lauren is second choice. This sense is reinforced by the fact that Bo and Lauren only engage in sexual relations twice, while Bo and Dyson have an extensive sexual relationship.

There is nothing inherently wrong with this. Many bisexuals choose a member of the opposite sex to settle down with for a variety of reasons. The problem with *Lost Girl* is that there's no explanation of why Bo so favours Dyson over Lauren. We don't see a deeper connection with one than the other, that Dyson is the better match for Bo either sexually or intellectually, the narrative is simply set up in such a way that it's evident Dyson is Bo's true love.

Lauren is the fragile woman Bo will inevitably hurt.

Dyson is literally the strong protector capable of healing Bo.

This does nothing to help the bisexual community shake the stigma that bisexuals are often fickle, incapable of commitment, and are at heart really straight people who play around with members of the opposite sex for fun, but nothing more meaningful.

The Anita Blake Series, by Laurel K. Hamilton

In many ways Laurel K. Hamilton's *Anita Blake Series* (1993-2016) pioneered Urban Fantasy. It has a lot to offer, and is certainly far more willing to portray LGBTQ characters than many other series. This is especially true considering the length of time the series has been running. *Guilty Pleasures* was published in 1993, long before the appearance of Sookie Stackhouse or *True Blood*, at a time when LGBTQ characters were still few and far between.

Despite this, the series is definitely a warning that quality should always trump quantity.

The inclusion of LGBTQ characters simply for the sake of representing them is not nearly as important as the *accurate* portrayal of different sexualities. *Anita Blake*'s LGBTQ cast are so steeped in stereotype they make *True Blood* seem positively realistic. Not only are the characters stereotyped, they are riddled with negative associations. The series includes four (arguably five) bisexuals who are villainous. With one exception (Asher), they are also sadistic rapists and/or murderers and torturers.

One of the only redeemable bisexuals in the series is Asher, a villain rescued by the indomitable Anita, who saves his soul and essentially straightens him out. This plays right into the stereotype that bisexuals are really straight people who haven't met 'the one' yet. There are additional villains in the series who are gay, rather than bisexual, and they too are rapists who seem to delight in forcing straight men to have gay sex.

While there are LGBTQ characters in the series on the side of good, the overwhelming message here is that bisexuals (even more so than gay people) are perverted, evil, and wrong. There is no saving them except by the love of a suitable person of the opposite sex who can put them back on the straight and narrow.

This poor impression is only furthered by Anita's men, all of whom are portrayed as being straight, but open to gay sex *if it pleases Anita.* While Anita engages in relationships with multiple male partners, their contact with each other is initially limited to avoid upsetting Anita. When Anita decides she enjoys watching men together, they suddenly pay more attention to each other.

Not because they are enjoying each other, but because *she* is enjoying *them.*

This is a much more extreme version of what we see on *True Blood*, where male-on-male encounters are perfectly acceptable for the viewing pleasure of the audience, but when they're related to plot or character development they're censored.

Jean-Claude is a main male character in the series who has a relationship with both Anita and Asher. The implication being that he is, like Asher, bisexual. Yet Hamilton goes to great pains to point out that Jean-Claude likes women, and Asher is an aberration. Many of the other male characters who engage in bisexual relationships are similarly 'explained' as being truly straight.

It would be remiss to exclude Anita herself from this list. Her sexual encounters are largely limited to men. The exception is Jade, the living embodiment of several terrible stereotypes: women are only lesbians because men have abused them; there must always be a subservient, weaker partner (which requires Jade to be minuscule, as Anita is already petite).

Other bisexual and lesbian characters in the series exist almost exclusively on the side of the villains.

Rather than being a series portraying the spectrum of sexuality, *Anita Blake* is a hornet's nest of stereotypes, misconceptions, and very negative implications. It fetishises male-on-male sex and presents it as voyeuristic titillation for the pleasure of Anita and/or the reader. While gay sex occurs in wild abandon, it's far from a realistic representation of gay and bisexual relationships. Female-on-female sex is very limited, and almost always expressed as a reaction to the mistreatment of the woman by men. The B-Bomb only gets dropped in reference to the villains of the series. Any bisexual activity on the side of Anita and the good guys is downplayed and referred to as something else entirely.

Asher is the only true exception to this and he's portrayed in a very negative light: insecure, pouting, prone to throwing tantrums, a consummate drama queen, and very fond of issuing emotional ultimatums. He's a manipulative egomaniac, who constantly requires reassurance and attention. He's possessive, jealous, frequently overwrought and drowning in angst. His relationships with men are very quickly side-lined in favour of Anita.

Asher is bisexual stereotyping at its finest.

Given that the gay men of the series are seen to be weak, naïve, and in every way inferior to the other 'real men', the series as a whole does nothing to further the LGBTQ cause despite its outward appearance of being a strong representation of it. This is made explicit by the werehyenas of the series. This bunch of characters had great potential. Their leader, Narcissus, is supposed to be intersex and gender-fluid. In reality, he's consistently referred to as male, and presented as a gay man who enjoys dressing as a woman, and refuses to allow women into his clan because they would threaten his leadership. The werehyena clan consists almost entirely of gay men, all of whom are portrayed as physically very attractive and muscly, yet somehow weak. They do not consist of fighters and are forced to bring in outside protection in the form of werewolves (i.e. the 'real men') to keep them safe.

The Kate Daniels Series, by Ilona Andrews

If we contrast this to the portrayal of bisexual characters, and the LGBTQ community in general, in another urban fantasy series, we see a marked difference. Ilona Andrews' *Kate Daniels* series (2007-2016) has a similar plethora of shapeshifting clans, one of which is clan 'bouda', a small group of extremely formidable shapeshifters. Unlike Hamilton's werehyenas, Andrews' male boudas are not afraid of women taking over, they are happily subservient to them: women rule the hyenas, that's the way of nature. This doesn't make the male hyenas weak, it simply makes their women phenomenally strong. Not only this, but Andrews portrays the hyenas as being sexually liberated. They enjoy multiple partners, have very strong sex drives, and when they do settle down love fiercely. It's suggested that most, if not all, are completely free when it comes to gender and happily partake in sex with both sexes. One character in particular is very well drawn, a bisexual bouda who simply discounts gender from the equations. She has a very minor role, with only a handful of lines, yet in her brief appearance she is presented as a strong, self-assured bisexual character who works hard, plays hard, and fiercely defends those weaker than herself, especially innocents. Not for money, or power, or fame, but simply because it's the right thing to do. The *Kate Daniels* novels are littered with LGBTQ characters, including the gay alpha leaders of clan rat, one of Kate's close friends and inner circle who is openly gay, and numerous characters who are minor to the plot but display very well-rounded and diverse preferences when it comes to sexuality, which go far beyond the realms of gay, straight, and bisexual.

In Kate's world, relationships are given equal weight and attention regardless of the sex, gender, orientation, or species of the parties involved.

The Shadowhunter Chronicles, by Cassandra Clare

Cassandra Clare is another urban fantasy author to tackle LGBTQ characters head on. There are at least four bisexual characters in her *Shadowhunter Chronicles* (2007-ongoing), including Magnus Band, Helen, Mark, and Michael Wayland. The author has spoken openly about her attempts to write inclusively and include diversity in her characters, yet she has also acknowledged that, 'I am aware I will screw up and make mistakes and I always appreciate questions that make me think' (Clare 2015). While the bisexual characters in the series are portrayed phenomenally well, the reaction of some of the other characters to their bisexuality is less than savoury.

Magnus Bane is, without doubt, one of the most iridescent portrayals of bisexual nature in recent Fantasy works. He's flamboyant and loveable, in some ways stereotypical, but only slightly. He has an edge of camp, but it's well-rounded out with other characteristics. He's slightly effeminate but in a way that indicates he embraces the full spectrum of his sexuality, rather than making him weaker than straight male characters, as is often the case; Magnus is far from weak in every respect.

The issue comes from Alec, a gay character in deep denial at the start of the series. He's in love with Jace but refuses to acknowledge it. He's attracted to Magnus but completely ignores it. When he finally accepts his feelings for Magnus, he remains very insecure about his sexuality and their relationship. This manifests in frequent cruel, spiteful, and offensive remarks concerning Magnus' bisexuality.

Alec sees bisexuality as an unpleasant, dirty business. Through his remarks, Alec uses stereotypical insults and slurs frequently levelled at the bisexual community. While it may be realistic to portray a character unsure of his own sexuality in this manner, the fact all the other characters let it slide is problematic.

Magnus is perfectly capable of defending himself and arguably chooses not to because he understands Alec's reasons. The others have no such excuse. They dismiss Alec's comments or simply ignore them, giving the impression they agree, or at least think they're reasonable.

It's difficult to accept such a glaring inconsistency in a series that is generally so good at portraying the LGBTQ community. It just goes to show that even when Fantasy authors get it absolutely right, they can still get some elements absolutely wrong.

Conclusion

Fantasy fiction is constantly evolving and changing, and there is no denying that a concerted effort is being made to include more and varied representations of bisexual characters. However, even a cursory look at bisexuality in Fantasy reveals extensive problems. Biphobia, bierasure, and stereotyping are prevalent, even in series that appear, at face value, to be incredibly inclusive.

The greatest sin of Fantasy literature is failing to allow bisexuals to speak for themselves, tell us how they feel, show us why they make decisions, and allow us to see the world from their viewpoint.

Understanding of gay and lesbian individuals has come on leaps and bounds in recent decades, due in large part to the increasingly adept portrayal of pivotal characters as gay or lesbian. Fiction gave these misunderstood minorities a voice, and they have greatly benefited from that. While it is evident that bisexual characters are on the rise, they are still lagging far behind. Too frequently, bisexual characters are absent, vague, bit parts, or stereotypes and caricatures. It's rare to find a bisexual character with a true voice in Fantasy.

While it is not true that all bisexual characters in Fantasy are nothing more than titillation for the audience, it is true, frequently enough, that the genuine bisexual characters are often tarred with the same ugly brush. Characters such as Magnus Bane and the LGBTQ denizens of Ilona Andrews' *Kate Daniels* novels are certainly self-assured, empowered characters embracing their true selves and their own sexuality. Yet beside them are stories that almost get it right, but miss the mark, like *True Blood* and *Lost Girl*, and those that are simply disturbing in their negativity, like Laurel K. Hamilton's *Anita Blake* series. Despite this criticism, we must remember the Anita Blake books began in the early 90s, a decade or more before those series we now look at and call progressive.

In only a decade we have come so far in our understanding and depiction of bisexuality in fiction. It may not yet be perfect, but it's certainly getting better.

And that's no small achievement.

Bibliography

Andrew, I., 2007. *Magic Bites*. New York: Ace Books.

Andrew, I., 2008. *Magic Burns*. New York: Ace Books.

Andrew, I., 2009. *Magic Strikes*. New York: Ace Books.

Andrew, I., 2010. *Magic Bleeds*. New York: Ace Books.

Andrew, I., 2011. *Magic Slays*. New York: Ace Books.

Andrew, I., 2012. *Gunmetal Magic*. New York: Ace Books.

Andrew, I., 2013. *Magic Rises*. New York: Ace Books.

Andrew, I., 2014. *Magic Breaks*. New York: Ace Books.

Andrew, I., 2015. *Magic Shifts*. New York: Ace Books.

Andrew, I., 2016. *Magic Binds*. New York: Ace Books.

Brown, R.M., 2011. *Write On*. [online] Available at: <http://www.huffingtonpost.com/rita-mae-brown/write-on_b_314361.html> [Accessed 5 March 2017].

Carey, J., 2001. *Kushiel's Dart*. New York: Tor Books.

Carey, J., 2002. *Kushiel's Chosen*. New York: Tor Books.

Carey, J., 2003. *Kushiel's Avatar*. New York: Tor Books.

Carey, J., 2006. *Kushiel's Scion*. New York: Tor Books.

Carey, J., 2007. *Kushiel's Justice*. New York: Tor Books.

Carey, J., 2008. *Kushiel's Mercy*. New York: Tor Books.

Carey, J., 2009. *Naamah's Kiss*. New York: Tor Books.

Carey, J., 2010. *Naamah's Curse*. New York: Tor Books.

Carey, J., 2011. *Naamah's Blessing*. New York: Tor Books.

Clare C., 2012. *City of Lost Souls*. London: Walker Books Ltd.

Clare, C., 2007. *City of Bones*. London: Walker Books Ltd.

Clare, C., 2008. *City of Ash*. London: Walker Books Ltd.

Clare, C., 2009. *City of Glass*. London: Walker Books Ltd.

Clare, C., 2011. *City of Fallen Angels*. London: Walker Books Ltd.

Clare, C., 2014a. *City of Heavenly Fire*. London: Walker Books Ltd.

Clare, C., 2014b. *The Bane Chronicles*. London: Walker Books Ltd.

Clare, C., 2015. *Bisexual Character in the Shadowhunter Series*. [online] Available at: <http://cassandraclare.tumblr.com/post/101512211199/bisexual-characters-in-the-shadowhunter-chronicles> [Accessed 6 March 2017].

Coulthurst, A., 2016. *Of Fire and Stars*. New York: Balzer & Bray/Harperteen.

Duyvis, C., 2014. *Otherbound*. New York: Amulet Books.

Hamilton, L.K., 2000. *Obsidian Butterfly*. New York: Ace Books.

Hamilton, L.K., 1993. *Guilty Pleasures*. New York: Ace Books.

Hamilton, L.K., 1994. *The Laughing Corpse*. New York: Ace Books.

Hamilton, L.K., 1995. *Circus of the Damned*. New York: Ace Books.

Hamilton, L.K., 1996. *Bloody Bones*. New York: Ace Books.

Hamilton, L.K. 1996b. *The Lunatic Cafe*. New York: Ace Books.

Hamilton, L.K., 1997. *The Killing Dance*. New York: Ace Books.

Hamilton, L.K., 1998. *Blue Moon*. New York: Ace Books.

Hamilton, L.K., 1998b. *Burnt Offerings*. New York: Ace Books.

Hamilton, L.K., 2001. *Narcissus in Chains*. New York: Ace Books.

Hamilton, L.K., 2003. *Cerulean Sins*. New York: Ace Books.

Hamilton, L.K., 2004. *Incubus Dreams*. New York: Ace Books.

Hamilton, L.K., 2006. *Danse Macabre*. New York: Ace Books.

Hamilton, L.K., 2007. *The Harlequin*. New York: Ace Books.

Hamilton, L.K., 2008. *Blood Noir*. New York: Ace Books.

Hamilton, L.K., 2009. *Skin Trade*. New York: Ace Books.

Hamilton, L.K., 2010. *Bullet*. New York: Ace Books.

Hamilton, L.K., 2011. *Hit List*. New York: Ace Books.

Hamilton, L.K., 2012. *Kiss the Dead*. New York: Ace Books.

Hamilton, L.K., 2013. *Affliction*. New York: Ace Books.

Hamilton, L.K., 2015. *Dead Ice*. New York: Ace Books.

Hamilton, L.K., 2016. *Crimson Death*. New York: Ace Books.

Hewett, E., 2014. *True Blood Season 7: WTF Has Happened to Jessica's Boyfriend*. [online] Available at: <http://metro.co.uk/2014/07/07/true-blood-season-7-wtf-has-happened-to-jessicas-boyfriend-james-4786766> [Accessed 5 March 2017].

Huff, T., 1991. *Blood Price*. London: Orbit.

Huff, T., 1992a. *Blood Trail*. London: Orbit.

Huff, T., 1992b. *Blood Lines*. London: Orbit.

Huff, T., 1993. *Blood Pact*. London: Orbit.

Huff, T., 1997. *Blood Debt*. London: Orbit.

Huff, T., 2015. *The Fire's Stone*. New York: Jabberwocky Literary Agency.

Lam, L., 2013. *Pantomime*. London: Pan.

Lam, L., 2014. *Shadowplay*. London: Pan.

Lam, L., 2015. *Masquerade*. London: Pan.

Lam, L., 2016. *False Hearts*. London: Macmillan.

Lost Girl 2010-2016. [TV programme] Canada: Prodigy Pictures.

Maas, S.J., 2012. *Throne of Glass*. London: Bloomsbury Children's.

Maas, S.J., 2013. *Crown of Midnight*. London: Bloomsbury Children's.

Maas, S.J., 2014. *Heir of Fire*. London: Bloomsbury Children's.

Maas, S.J., 2015. *Queen of Shadows*. London: Bloomsbury Children's.

Maas, S.J., 2016. *Empire of Storms*. London: Bloomsbury Children's.

Nichols, J., 2016. *Anna Paquin Declares She Is A 'Happily Married Bisexual Mother*. [online] Available at: < http://www.huffingtonpost.com/2014/06/11/anna-paquin-bisexual-mother_n_5484365.html> [Accessed 5 March 2017].

Selby, J., 2015. *Anna Paquin Answers Larry King's Ridiculous Line of Questioning About Her Bisexuality*. [online] Available at: < http://www.independent.co.uk/news/people/anna-paquin-answers-larry-kings-ridiculous-line-of-questioning-about-her-bisexuality-9648876.html> [Accessed 5 March 2017].

Sim, T., 2016. *Timekeeper*. New York: Sky Pony Press.

Stiefvater, M., 2012. *The Raven Boys*. New York: Scholastic.

Stiefvater, M., 2013. *The Dream Thieves*. New York: Scholastic.

Stiefvater, M., 2014. *Blue Lily, Lily Blue*. New York: Scholastic.

Stiefvater, M., 2015. *The Raven King*. New York: Scholastic.

True Blood, 2008-2014. [TV programme] US: HBO.

Doll Parts: Reflections of the Feminine Grotesque in Frances Hardinge's *Cuckoo Song* and Neil Gaiman's *Coraline*

By Kim Lakin-Smith

Neil Gaiman's titular Coraline knows that something lurks on the far side of a locked door while, in Cuckoo Song, Frances Hardinge's anti-heroine Not-Triss is haunted by a sense that she is ill - or wrong - 'quailing to see her own face staring in from the night.' On the bleeding edge of adulthood, these strange little girls are ravenous for the forbidden fruits of self-sovereignty, sexual maturity and knowledge. But in shrugging off their shrink-wrap, are they remade as that ultimate female pariah, the menstruating doll? Using Lacan's psychoanalytical study of the 'Mirror Image' stage and David Elkind's theory on 'Egocentrism in Adolescence,' this paper seeks to explore the arcane nature of the 'feminine grotesque,' and identifies three aspects - Doll Child, Wild Woman and Other Mother. Both Coraline and Cuckoo Song lend themselves to Simone de Beauvoir's The Second Sex and Julia Kristeva's essay on abjection and the female 'other', through which we find a fresh understanding of predatorial parents, societal gatekeepers, paedophilic patriarchs, and 'the monster' in the mirror. It is my proposal that these domestic fairy tales restructure the doll parts of the feminine grotesque to reflect a state of 'real girl' consciousness.

"*What would they do if she transformed herself before their eyes into a child-eating monster, a creature of the darkest fairy-tale?*" (Hardinge, 2014:289) asks anti-heroine, Not-Triss, in Frances Hardinge's 2014 Carnegie Medal shortlisted novel *Cuckoo Song*. By way of reply, the strapline for Neil Gaiman's 2002 Carnegie Medal winning Coraline declares, "*Sometimes, a door is closed for a very good reason.*" In truth, few things in this world provoke such profound feelings of fear and revulsion as the pubescent girl. With her bodily emissions, engendered sexuality and hunger for forbidden knowledge, this feminine grotesque is all things dark and dangerous. The adolescent girl is historically 'unhinged' – or, as psychoanalysis would have it, burdened with penial lack and driven frantic with self-loathing. She grubs in wastelands, joins in with the Wild Hunt, outwits fire, survives frost, unlocks doors, and straddles and crosses borders – precisely the social perversities that underpin *Cuckoo Song* and *Coraline*.

While contemporary young adult fiction is heavily populated with female robin hoods and urban warriors, there is a subtlety to the ab(normal)ity of growing up as a girl which is best illustrated via these domestic fairy-tales. Holding up a fun house mirror to the real world, Hardinge and Gaiman explore and expose a freak show of gender expectation, where mother is other, girls are manufactured dolls, made to devour and be devoured, and womanhood is a wilderness society strives to tame. This process of organic and psychological reordering lends both texts to a Lacanian ideal of spatial identification and primordial discord[1].

---

1. Jacques Marie Émile Lacan was a French psychoanalyst and psychiatrist who proposed the concept of 'The Mirror Stage' in psychoanalytic development. In Lacan's fourth Seminar, *La relation d'objet*, he describes the formation of the Ego via the process of identification, the Ego resulting from the subject identifying with one's own specular image. He posits that infants recognise themselves in a mirror (literal) or other

By focusing on the oscillations of the female adolescent, Gaiman and Hardinge provide powerful feminist testaments on the fragmentation of self and societal mothering. Their stories highlight three aspects of the female construct - Doll Child, Wild Woman, and Other Mother – reflecting that unholy trinity of feminine grotesques, the maiden, whore, and crone. Through the deconstruction and reassembly of stock characters, these authors create real girls beyond the mirror image.

To demarcate the bleeding edge, as it were, of female adolescence, it is helpful to refer to child psychologist, David Elkind's theory of 'Adolescent Egocentrism.' Centring on the 11-to-13-year-old age group, Elkind describes a phenomenon where young adolescents display an inability to distinguish between their perception of what others think about them and what people think in reality (1967). This psychosis gives rise to two mental constructs – the Imaginary Audience, whereby the adolescent anticipates the reactions of those around him/her in current or impending situations and avoids this fantasy of scrutiny, and Personal Fable, where the individual takes on the belief that his/her feelings are unique and that they are therefore unique and

---

symbolic apparatus that can be viewed by the child outside of themselves from the age of six months. His theory proposes the notions of 'Historical value' - the mental development of the child - and 'structural value' - relating to the libidinal relationship with the body image. He states that "the mirror stage is far from a mere phenomenon which occurs in the development of the child. It illustrates the conflictual nature of the dual relationship." This dual relationship extends from ego and the body to the relation between the Imaginary and the Real. Identifying with the reflection in the mirror supplies the subject with imaginary 'wholeness' even while experiencing a fragmentary reality.

special. It is this duality, posits Elkind, which shapes the young adolescent's sense of self.

But, what happens if the female adolescent realises that she is not just an outsider, but an imposter? Finding herself made the *wrong* side of the mirror, Hardinge's antiheroine can't help but attract scrutiny. As Triss's younger sister, the wild and adventurous Pen, snaps, "You're getting everything just a bit wrong...sooner or later, they'll notice." (Hardinge, 2014:40). The paranoia of Elkind's immature adolescent is inverted because 'Not-Triss' turns out to be a golem, stitched together from twigs, litter and feathers. As such we must accept that her paranoia is the very mirror image of imagined; it is real. A living doll, Not-Triss must un-learn her reflected self in order to separate from the 'Trissness closing around her like damp swaddling clothes.' (64). Likewise, Not Triss *is* special precisely because of her lack of definition. She can leap between buildings, issue a monstrous cry, and eat and eat – everything from rotten windfalls to china dolls to pieces of her own dress. A motherless pariah, she longs to be whole but, no matter how much she devours, the hunger still howls inside.

The titular Coraline is far more self-assured, but no less cosseted. While Not-Triss's false parents, Mr and Mrs Crescent, supplement their grief for the loss of their son in the war with caring for their eldest daughter whose 'job' it is to be ill, Coraline is domestically independent but denied freedom of expression. The bright green gloves she craves in the clothes shop are a signature of her lust to embrace the Personal Fable and separate herself from the herd; "But mum," she pleads, "I could be the only one." (Gaiman, 2002:29). But when Coraline's mother sides with the shop assistant and buys the standard school uniform, the message is clear; Coraline is not special. Even when she steals a key placed out of reach and unlocks the spare door in the pristine drawing room onto a (warped) mirror image of her reality, it is Coraline's not-specialness which helps her see through the glamour. The gift of the protection stone from Miss Spink and Miss Forcible is both reminder that these women thirst after the cultural freedom of theatrical careers cut short by the female crimes of spinsterhood and ageing, and that she must embrace her burgeoning sexuality and look through the stone's hole to see the 'truth.'

Truth, however, is not always comfortable or welcome. In choosing autonomy over the indulgent suppression of the other mother's playhouse, Coraline is gifted a last vestige of childhood – a dream where she plays with the ghost children she has rescued: "They just laughed and ran in a game that was partly tag, partly piggy-in-the-middle, and partly a magnificent romp." (171). Coraline teeters between the child id she recognises in the mirror and a new reality where she must shrug off childhood things and embrace her adult ego. When her parents are kidnapped by her Other Mother, she does her best to imitate adulthood – completing a supermarket shop for apples and livid-green limeade, microwaving frozen pizza, cleaning her teeth without being asked, and putting herself to bed. But this self-parenting is make-believe; incapable of feeding herself properly, Coraline climbs into her parents' bed at night and cries herself to sleep. Seesawing between truth and loss, she repeatedly tells adults that she is an 'explorer', seeking adventure beyond her front door. But she also craves the mundanity of parental love and (societal) rules:

> *She hugged her mother, so tightly that her arms began to ache. Her mother hugged her back. "Dinner in fifteen minutes," said her mother. "Don't forget to wash your hands. And just look at those pyjama bottoms. What did you do to your poor knee?"* (167)

Cuckoo Song's Not-Triss also suffers a juxtaposition between dissolution and reassembly of self. Hers, however, is a physical degradation of organism alongside a cerebral shift in recognition:

> *(She) grabbed at a few strands of her own hair, yanked them out, hardly feeling the pain, and held them up. Within seconds, she could feel them changing in her grip, becoming dry and crumbling. Then the wind was teasing fragments of filigree leaf from between her fingers...*
> *"I'm falling apart!" Triss could hear all her anguish escaping her voice, making it so harsh she barely recognised it. "Why is this happening to me?"*
> (Hardinge, 2014:115)

Not-Triss experiences the onset of pubescence as a devolution, a fracturing. Against the patriarchal nest of her comfortable, middle class home life, Not Triss's erosion of self is viewed as 'wrong', and 'ill', aka perverse. The physical disintegration of Hardinge's golem girl aligns with the advent of female puberty, when the abject wound of menstruation mars the pristine Doll Child. Not-Triss complains, "The pain was shocking, but worse was the dizzy weakness that followed, the sense of having lost part of her very self." (213). A universal repulsion to womanhood is given expression through society's response to menstruation, from biblical warnings against associating with those women who are 'unclean' to the language of a 'woman's problem' and 'the curse'. As writer and philosopher, Simone de Beauvoir, acknowledges, in her seminal study, *The Second Sex*:

> *This blood is a manifestation of her impurity; it appears when the woman can be fertile; when it disappears, she becomes sterile again; it pours forth from this womb where the foetus is made. The horror of feminine fertility that man experiences is expressed through it.* (Beauvoir, 2009:169)

To accept the ascribed grotesqueness of female maturity is to acknowledge the pristine model of pre-pubescence. Beauvoir sees society's reading of the adolescent doll as a problem of misidentification and phallocentrism. She asserts that boys take pride in their sexual organs, which they view physically as both apart from and a part of themselves, forming a sense of identity independent of the sex organs. Conversely, girls are perceived as lacking because their sex organs are internal. Demonstrating an indifferent attitude towards the clitoris, girls are forced to identify inseparably with their sex, which, in turn, leads boys to think of women in this manner. The gift of a doll lends the little girl an alter ego to identify with in the same way that a little boy identifies with his genitals. Beauvoir writes:

> *It is a figurine with a human face—or a corn husk or even a piece of wood—that will most satisfyingly replace this double, this natural toy, this penis. The great difference is that, on the one hand, the doll represents the whole body and, on the other hand, it is a passive thing. As such, the little girl will be encouraged to alienate herself in her person as a whole and to consider it an inert given. While the boy seeks himself in his penis as an autonomous subject, the little girl pampers her doll and dresses her as she dreams of being dressed and pampered; inversely, she thinks of herself as a marvelous doll.* (340)

The notion of girl-as doll pervades *Cuckoo Song*. Not-Triss remembers the formation of her former self, how she was primed with new party dresses – '…her whooping cough blue. Her three day fever with the primrose print,' (Hardinge, 2014:54) - and even removed from school where she was in danger of thriving – in other words, sated by the forbidden fruit of knowledge enjoyed by Eve, patriarchy's very first doll, and quested after by Pen, 'That little snake.' (42). Not-Triss struggles to maintain her namesake's (in)validity; losing weight, or substance, her insatiable hunger leads her into acts of self-devouring. She turns on one of the china dolls which has been her silent partner in placidity:

> *…the half-doll was making a faint musical noise, like the sound of cups tottering on saucers. Its jaw was moving rapidly up and down, but she could not tell whether it was cackling, gnashing its teeth or trying to talk.*

> *"Stop it! Hissed Triss... "Stop it, or I'll...eat you!*
> *The little doll's voice increased to a crockery snarl.*
> *A black well of terror swallowed Triss. She closed her*
> *eyes and opened her mouth wide, then wider.*
> *The china slid over her tongue like ice cream.* (77)

This cannibalism of the doll self is echoed throughout. In Not-Triss's dream, Pen cries with glee, "Triss ate the ceilings!..Triss ate the walls!" (85) - betraying her older sister's desire to disintegrate the family home with its associations of domesticity, pre-moulded femininity and marriage. In the ultimate test of self-annihilation, Not-Triss learns that she may live beyond seven days if she eats Pen: '...her not-sister was full of unspent years, like pips in a robust little apple.' (354). That Not-Triss is able to resist despite the fact 'there was a hole inside her like a bottomless shaft that a person might just tumble into,' (315) inverts the ascribed wildness of woman - societally, that most problematic of female aspects.

As Hardinge's righteous inquisitor, Mr Grace, avows "Thorns for teeth. Yes, that's its real appearance. Sometimes they revert when they're frightened or angry." (167). After the organic sterility of the doll child, Not-Triss deconstructs into the unfettered, organic entity of the wild woman. 'Her instincts prickled in her veins like a thousand tiny thorns, causing her muscles to tense and coil,' (137) while 'The wind rose and became bitingly chill. (She) could feel it starting to tear her apart like a dandelion clock.' (304). Likewise, Coraline starts out as the Other Mother's plaything; she is momentarily seduced by delicious tea parties, fantastical toy chests, dogs (always a child's best friend) who eat 'forbidden' chocolates (which Coraline gives away) and the circus tricks of Miss Spink and Miss Forcible grown young. But Coraline sees too much; in refusing to replace her eyes with buttons like the Others on the far side of the door, she is untamed by the Other Mother's idealised definitions and forced to fend for herself amongst, and against, the wild things. "We were here before you fell, you will be here when we rise," (Gaiman, 2002:38) sing a chorus of rats Coraline is sent to play with, calling to mind the Fall of Eve. Determined to escape the Other adults - those repressive automatons - Coraline joins her fellow rebel/familiar, the cat, in exploring the outer limits of the alternative reality. Beyond woods that are more 'like the idea of trees: a greyish-brown trunk below a greenish splodge,' (85) Coraline investigates a none-space beyond the wilds: 'The world she was walking through was a pale nothingness, like a blank sheet of paper or an enormous, empty white room. It had no temperature, no smell, no texture, and no taste.' (86). This space is the Unwritten, a decoded coda, a nothing the knowing self cannot comprehend. It is the purity and the impossibility of a mirror that has nothing to reflect, where all archetypes erase.

Not-Triss's familiar surroundings are similarly erased when unseasonal snow falls across the town of Ellchester in September. But this whited world is the construct of Violet Parish, fiancé of Triss's dead brother (aka 'war hero') who is forever on the run to escape the Winter of her Discontent. Outside of Wild White Week, 'when the usual rules had temporarily stopped working,' (Hardinge, 2014:398) Not-Triss's monstrous pubescence is exposed as chaos versus order, 'a twisted labyrinth of her own mind,' (316) where self fractures and reality bites. As Violet confides,

> *"...you woke up one day and found that you couldn't be the person you remembered being, the little girl everybody expected you to be. You just weren't her any more, and there was nothing you could do about it. So your family decided you were a monster and turned on you."* (294)

Violet understands that her 'duty' is to be weak, wane and emotionally dependent on Mr and Mrs Crescent - not unlike human poppet, Triss, who was shaped by their paternal nursing. Except, Violet doesn't need or want to be consoled. Hers is a 'fast' world; she parties unescorted, listens to jazz 'that had not wiped its feet' (183), stays out all night, rides a motorcycle, and is unconventionally supportive but none-maternal to the two young girls in her care. Little wonder she frightens Not-Triss when the golem girl is still in denial of her wild origins:

> *Violet had indeed seemed cold – cold, selfish and ugly. Her visit had ripped a hole in the fragile calm of the house...She had seen herself through Violet's eyes, a pallid, simpering accomplice of her father's claims.* (69)

In contrast, Pen demonstrates 'an occasional perverse insistence that she liked Violet.' (71). While Not-Triss clings to the self-validity of her place in the Crescent family, Pen is the square peg in a round hole, the knowing rebel who will not listen, or rationalise, or quieten. It is Pen who feeds her true sister to the wolves when she makes a lethal bargain with the chief Besider, the alluring Architect, Pen who is addicted to Gangster movies, 'and any other picture that involved people shooting each other or falling off cliffs,' (97) and Pen who is seen '…strutting down Lime Street as if she had every right to do so.' (95). As Not-Triss observes, Pen is precisely the kind of wild child who will break open life 'with a new and fierce curiosity.' (108). Pen, and Violet too, represent a new generation of women post-war, adventurers who earn their way, thrive independently of marriage, and who, as Violet remarks, can '…move towards something, instead of just running…' (400).

In the ultimate act of patriarchal rebellion, the wild woman has the ability to redefine and rename herself, quite literally in the case of Not-Triss. Sacrificing the name necklace Pen gave to her, 'Trista' feeds it into the inner workings of her dead brother's watch, releasing his ghost from the Architect's snare and, at the same time, solidifying her new born sense of self. Inversely, a name can be stolen, and with it, the power/identity of the victim. Coraline wants desperately to find her place beyond the boredom of domestic mundanity. But as with taking on any quest, there is danger. When her Other Mother forces her through the hallway mirror into the coffin-like cupboard beyond, Coraline encounters the trapped souls of children who have already been devoured:

> … *"Art thou – art thou alive?"*
> *"Yes," whispered Coraline.*
> *"Poor child," said the first voice.*
> *"Who are you?" whispered Coraline.*

> *"Names, names, names," said another voice, all faraway and lost. "The names are the first things to go, after the breath has gone, and the beating of the heart."* (Gaiman, 2002:98)

The familiar adage holds true; to name a thing is to gain dominion over it. A name signifies power, individuality and substance. It is heavily invested with a subject's sense of self, as illustrated when Coraline first meets the cat:

> *"What's your name,' Coraline asked the cat. 'Look, I'm Coraline. Okay?'*
> *'Cats don't have names,' it said.*
> *'No?' said Coraline.*
> *'No,' said the cat. 'Now you people have names. That's because you don't know who you are. We know who we are, so we don't need names."* (45)

To lose one's identity can be read at a deeper, psychological level, where it is to regress inside the mother and reduce to foetal malleability. From the Other Mother's spiderish right-hand tumbling into the gloomy shaft of the real life well to the shifting sentience of the corridor between reality and the Other place, the threat is *reabsorption* into the maternal body, a swallowing up, an un-birthing. In place of a more abstract notion of the feminine grotesque, fear is realised as textured and synesthetic. As abject.

In *Powers of Horror* (1982), feminist, philosopher and psychoanalyst, Julia Kristeva ascribes this reflux to a 'primal' rupturing of the "I" (ego) from the mother 'Other.' She writes, 'Abjection preserves what existed in the archaism of pre-objectal relationship, in the immemorial violence with which a body becomes separated from another body in order to be.' (10). A subject's anathema to the maternal host is the dread of being *un*-born. To access the fantastical world and then to escape it, Coraline must pass through a dark corridor of something 'very old and very slow.' (Gaiman, 2002:33) With its furred and wet walls, this birth canal is at once stale and cold, limber and alive. It is the umbilical cord linking un-being to being, a borderland where life and death are braided.

Not-Triss navigates a similar corridor between the real balcony wall in the cinema and the fantastical world of the Architect's office on the reverse:

> *The carpet crunched strangely under (Not) Triss's feet as she advanced down the corridor, soft but prickly, delicate but fibrous. The wallpaper looked a lot like velvet with some of its pile shaved to create patterns. When she put her hand out to touch it, however, she found her fingertips stroking feathers. As she brushed the wall, a tiny tremor seemed to flutter through the pattern, as though the wall was a living thing and had stirred its plumage.* (Hardinge, 2014:101)

This vagina dentata, from whose suckering grasp Not-Triss must pull the monochromatic, voiceless Pen, reoccurs when the golem girl swaps places with the kidnapped Triss. Believing he is burying her namesake alive, the Architect forces Not-Triss into the gaping hole of the pyramid at the newly completed station, there to await the 'Capping

Ceremony.' Threatened with reabsorption into the other world of the Besiders, Not-Triss inverts the role of victim when she reveals herself. The Architect gives 'another terrible, infantile shriek' (391) and, losing 'control of himself', falls into 'the dark, abysmal shaft' (392) at the heart of the room. After, Not-Triss emerges from the open hole 'dripping and dishevelled' (398) – not un-born, but *re*-born.

Gaiman, meanwhile, takes reabsorption to its abject edge with his monsters-in-gestation. When Coraline finds the Other Miss Spink and Miss Forcible suspended in what reminds her of a spider's egg-case, she notices, 'The creature in the sac seemed horribly unformed and unfinished, as if two Plasticine people had been warmed and rolled together, squashed and pressed into one thing.' (Gaiman, 2002:119). Fearful of the threat of gestational regression, Coraline realises she has never been so scared as when she slips her hand into 'the sticky, clinging whiteness' (120) to retrieve the marble containing a ghost child's soul.

Psychoanalyst and psychiatrist, Jacques Lacan, addresses this fear of self-devolution in his theories on the 'imago' – which he identifies as responsible for establishing a relationship between the organism and its reality. Here, Lacan identifies 'a certain dehiscence (is) at the heart of the organism….a primordial Discord' which relates to 'humoral residues of the maternal organism.' (Lacan, 2001:505) Ever provocative in his theorising, Lacan regurgitates the claim that mother is 'other' – a corporal corruption from which the infant can only cleansed via baptism or psychoanalysis. The mother is abject because she spins a web of menses, traps the fly-like sperm, and weaves a golem.

Under this prescriptive regime, the mother is beyond bestial, she is insectile, that most abject organism which feasts on the corpse. The predatorial Other Mother, whose 'cold arms enfold her,' (Gaiman, 2002:70) like a spider cocooning its prey, repulses Coraline,. As the cat warns, "She wants something to love…Something that isn't her. She might want something to eat as well. It's hard to tell with creatures like that." (76). While the Other Mother temporarily makes do with crunching up a bag of beetles like sweets, Hardinge's golem girl feasts on windfalls and their resident pupa. She weeps spider-silk because she is fashioned of dead and abandoned things. In contrast, her 'mother', Celeste Crescent, is a pinnacle of sterility. Like the china dolls she plies Triss with, Celeste hides her emotions behind 'suitably feminine' behaviour, eats with appropriate reserve, does not raise her voice, and abandons her wild daughter to the literal fire of an all-male inquisition. In fact, Celeste is phobic of her suppressed wilderness. She objects to the 'bug huts' of cinemas with 'all sorts' (Hardinge, 2014:97) spreading fleas, and her room is pristine with 'soft lavender-coloured curtains' and 'smells of powder, potpourri and the slightly acrid scent of wine tonic.' (319)

There are hints at Celeste's inner monster. Not-Triss remembers seeing her father wrap his arms around her mother many times, 'gently and firmly, as if he holding together a broken thing long enough for the glue to set.' (161). As Kristeva assets, societal repulsion is exasperated by the 'humours' of motherhood, but inherent to being female:

It is thus not lack of cleanliness or health that

causes abjection but what disturbs identity, system, order. What does not respect borders, positions, rules. The in-between, the ambiguous, the composite. (Kristeva, 1982:4)

To restore the natural order, the mother is pupated into a new role – as guardian angel of the very order which both reveres and abhors her. Deemed 'untouchable,' she is placed upon a pedestal to overview the nanny state. This notion of societal mothering underpins Hardinge's use of the *scissors* motif. Not-Triss and her fellow Besiders are in mortal danger of scissors, 'intended for one job alone – snipping things in two. Dividing by force. Everything on one side or the other, and nothing in between. Certainty." (Hardinge, 2014:228). Under maternal law, scissors are representative of female sexuality. Ladies keep their legs crossed, never open. Violet, however, wears divided skirts and legs visible almost up to the knee. Her punishment for sexual sedition, and taking up a man's job beyond the exceptional circumstances of war, is to be gossiped about by older women – those territorial lynchpins of the patriarchal status quo – and forced to crash on her motorcycle, since 'Violet without her motorcycle was Violet with her wings clipped.' (345)

Not-Triss is similarly invalidated when Celeste Crescent cries,

> *"You little monster, what have you done with her? Where's my little girl?"*
> *"Mother…" With a sick feeling in her stomach, Not-Triss could feel her mouth drooping into the little sob-shape that always worked, that always*

made everybody soften and look after her. But it was a stolen mannerism, and today it only made things worse. (168)

The hole of female mis("I")dentification is cast as something that can only be filled by belonging. But when Celeste rejects Not-Triss, it is the maternally unencumbered Violet who steps in to give the golem girl substance:

Thank you. Trista mouthed the words, but could not give them voice. Thank you for coming to rescue me. More than anything else, it was the way Violet had called Trista her daughter that set Trista's eyes prickling. It made her feel that she had something small, fragile and warm to hold on to, something to put in the hole left by the fragments that the wind had chased across the roofs. (303)

That the pubescent female can achieve totality outside the prescribed roles of daughter, wife and mother is abject to Celeste and her fellow custodians. Likewise, the manner in which Coraline's Other Mother collects children like dolls to nourish her can be read as totemic of the social order. However, as is always the case with the wild woman, there is a cut-off point at which, "In the other mother's button eyes, Coraline knew that she was a possession, nothing more. A tolerated pet, whose behaviour was no longer amusing." (Gaiman, 2002:126). Not-Triss understands this division all too well: "She saw everything through a filter of her own strangeness and wildness. The familiar did not welcome her. It stared at her aghast." (Hardinge, 2014:318).

As has always been the norm across historical and cultural divides, whenever a woman steps outside the societal norm, she is branded that most abject of female aspects: a witch.

Gaiman's Other Mother is labelled a 'Beldam', a mythic witch figure defined as a 'malicious or loathsome old woman'[2]. With her long, wizen bones, clawed hand, and fragment of beetle stuck to her lower lip, Coraline tells her Other Mother, "You're sick...Sick and evil and weird," (Gaiman, 2002:91) – and so vocalises her abjection to the Beldam's repugnant consumption, but also genuflecting societal and ageist prejudice. Prowling the outer reaches of chaos and leeching life from the young, the Beldam is emblematic of the 'crone' archetype. Having lured Coraline in with treats, she pushes the young girl through the hallway mirror into the cupboard – direct homage to the witch of *Hansel and Gretel*, who lures the lost children with her gingerbread house, only to enslave Gretel to domesticity and cage Hansel, ready to be fattened and devoured. "She kept us, and she fed on us," the ghost children warn Coraline, "...until now we're nothing left of ourselves, only snakeskins and spider-husks." (101)

Hardinge does not run so easily towards the crone mythos. In *Cuckoo Song*, it is anti-heroine, Not-Triss, whose wild witch origins are exposed by the trickery of her inquisitors. Threatened with fire and echoing the pleas of outcast women across the centuries, Not-Triss appeals to her father, "He's wrong! I'm real! I'm real, and if you put me on the fire I'll die!" (Hardinge, 2014:170). It is Piers Crescent, and not the mother figure of Celeste, who is pivotal to this

---

2. English Oxford Living Dictionary.

attempted act of filicide. Here Hardinge raises her feminist colours, drawing a clear demarcation between maternal 'lack' and patriarchal law. Breaking into the Crescent home, Not-Triss is discovered by Piers, '…a tiny, miserable flame of hope ignited in his eyes,' (320) causing her to '…bare her thorn-teeth in a hiss. Her mind was a furnace. All thought singed and sizzled to nothingness.' (321). But Not-Triss has no intention of cooling her heels; she takes the fire inside and uses it to scorch the patriarchal Voice. "You're a loving father, but you're blind. Blind enough to be cruel," (322) she cries - and while blaming both parents for burying the real Triss alive with their need, it is Piers who must swallow her 'bitter taste of truth.' (324). In the ultimate triumph of the feminine grotesque over her beloved oppressor, Piers is reduced to other: 'Trista listened, and all the while, the part of her that was Triss sobbed to hear her father sounding so humble, abject and destroyed.' (327)

Unlike Triss and her corseted ilk in *Cuckoo Song*, Coraline is free to explore and think and imagine within the realms of reasonable parental guidelines. But her father has morphed into something inert and featureless which just will not play with her. Likewise, her Other Father is increasingly revealed as a malleable golem forced to exact the Other Mother's will. In a similar inversion to how Trista feels about Piers when he finally breaks down, Coraline finds herself pitying this imperfect Other Father: '"Poor thing," she said. "You're just a thing she made and then threw away."' (Gaiman, 2002:132)

However, so too can we read the presence of a far darker, transgressive father figure. It is no accident that, bar the final showdown with her Other Mother, Coraline's last encounter on the far side of the door is with the corrupted mirror image of the Old Man who lives upstairs. Echoing aeons of parental warnings against bogeymen and strangers offering sweets, the Other Old Man squats in the gloom, promising new worlds to explore, where "Everyday will be better and brighter than the one that went before." (142). It is inherent self-protection which makes Coraline ill at ease in his presence: 'She wished she had a stick or something to poke him with; she had no wish to get any closer to the shadowy man at the end of the room.' (143). Reading from the archetypal script, the paedophile offers up that most abject of soothing pleas, "Come here, little girl. I know what you want, little girl." (141)

The sexual predator in Coraline is revealed as a mound of black rats – those skittering furred testes with penial tails. In reality, it is the revelation of the old man's name, Mister Bobo, which deflates any perceived/real threat, reiterating the adage that to name a thing is to gain dominion over it. As the newly named Trista tells her maker and 'father,' the architect. "You lost that game. I'm not your tool, and I never will be. I'm free and I'm myself, until my pieces fall into the gutter." (Hardinge, 2014:317)

Doll Child, Wild Woman, Other Mother – the pubescent female might be at odds with her reflected (fractured) self, but ultimately, she is the new world order, representing chaos bleeding into order, dark that encroaches on light, and corpse and cadaver beetle in symbiotic cohabitation. As Not-Triss dreams, 'Perhaps illness could be left behind, just like small, badly concealed china corpses.' (25). Triss and Pen re-join their parents, but the family unit has grown into 'new and unexpected shapes.' (402). Violet, too, is free to move or stand still in a world that is 'breaking and changing, and dancing.' (409). As for newborn Trista, she is so much more than a live Pinocchio, tucked up in the arms of a custodial parent. She is the self-governing wild child, a 'Peter Pan but with teeth.' (408). Equally, as the unregulated hedonism of her Other life collapse in on itself like the stage set it is, Coraline assumes the mantle of saviour over explorer. She is brave though she does not feel it, strong in collaboration with the ghost children and her parents' voices against the beldam, and ultimately at peace as the summer of her childhood draws to a close. The last vestiges of the fantastical world peeled away, Coraline is finally seen through others' eyes as 'extraordinary.' (Gaiman, 2002:191). In both texts, Hardinge and Gaiman reflect the societal and psychological complexities of real pubescent girls. Far from problematic, these feminine grotesques are signifiers of a substantial truth beyond the plasticity. They are doll parts, made whole.

Bibliography

Beauvoir de, S., 2009. *The Second Sex*. Translated from French by C. Borde and S. Malovany-Chevallier. New York. Vintage Books.

Elkind, D., 1967. Egocentrism in Adolescence. *Child Development*. Wiley, on behalf of the Society for Research in Child Development, Vol 38, no. 4.

English Oxford Living Dictionary, 2017. *Beldam*. [online] Available at: <https://en.oxforddictionaries.com/definition/beldam> [Accessed 17 January 2017]

Gaiman, N., 2002. *Coraline*. London. Bloomsbury.

Hardinge, F., 2014. *Cuckoo Song*. London. Macmillan Children's Books.

Kristeva, J., 1982. *Power of Horror: An Essay on Abjection*. Translated from French by L.S. Roudiez. New York. Columbia University Press.

Lacan, J., 2001. *The Mirror Stage as Formative of the Function of the I as Revealed in Psychoanalytic Experience*. Translated from French by A. Sheridan. London. Routledge, 2001.

McCallum, P., 1985. New Feminist Readings: Woman as Ecriture or Woman as Other. *Canadian Journal of Political and Social Theory* 9, nos. 1-2, Canada.

Muller, V., 2012. Same Old 'Other' Mother'?: Neil Gaiman's Coraline. *Outskirts*, Vol. 26, Perth.

Rudd, D., 2008. An Eye for an I: Neil Gaiman's Coraline and Questions of Identity. *Children's Literature in Education*: Vol. 39, International.

Subversion, Sex, and Violence: Rape as Narrative Tool in '*A Song of Ice and Fire*'

By Lorianne Reuser

Sexual violence is a pervasive part of American media, from news reports to prime time soap operas to cable programming. The concept of female body as object is entrenched in the visual imagery of popular culture, and the violated female body acts as a versatile narrative tool. Using previous critical scholarship on feminism and rape culture, along with essay collections devoted to George R.R. Martin's books and the ensuing HBO adaptation, I will examine the pervasive threat of sexual violence, with a focus on instances of rape, in Martin's and HBO's Westeros. In examining three controversial scenes of rape from the television adaptation -- namely those of Daenerys, Sansa, and Cersei -- and how they act in dialogue with the source text, I will explore how Martin uses rape as a means to subvert the type of fantasy that he calls a 'Disneyland Middle Ages', and concurrently how those specific scenes struggle to escape the tropes of current rape culture and its damaging effects on women and their experiences.

Though originally conceived as a series of books first published in 1996, George R.R. Martin's *A Song of Ice and Fire* exploded into popular culture consciousness with HBO's television series adaptation, *Game of Thrones*, in 2011 (hereafter referred to as *GoT*). Led by showrunners David Benioff and D.B. Weiss, and following in the footsteps of HBO's *Rome*, *Game of Thrones* continues to provoke controversy almost equivalent to its popularity. Blatant sex and brutal violence, so fundamental to HBO aesthetics, are ubiquitous in *GoT*, but they are also fundamental to Martin's subversion of typical fantasy tropes (Peterson, 2015:17). Martin has repeatedly positioned his work in opposition to J.R.R. Tolkien's *The Lord of the Rings* (1954) and the type of fantasy fiction that followed in its wake, reacting, as he says in an interview with EW's James Hibberd, against the "'Disneyland Middle Ages'.... [with its] princes and princesses and knights in shining armor ... [but without] ... what those societies meant and how they functioned" (2015). Rape, in particular, acts as a "particularly versatile narrative element" (Projansky, 2001:3) that Martin and the HBO showrunners employ to subvert the standard impression of fantasy worlds as lacking in realistic brutality. In the aforementioned EW interview, Martin explicitly states the necessity for rape's inclusion in his texts: "I'm writing about war ... But if you're going to write about war, and you just want to include all the cool battles and heroes killing a lot of orcs and things ... and you don't portray [sexual violence], then there's something fundamentally dishonest about that" (2015). The threat of rape is certainly a defining feature of *A Song of Ice and Fire*, and Benioff and Weiss have translated that looming threat into their adaptation through multiple scenes of violence against women. Between the books and the so-far six seasons of episodes, there are simply too many scenes and characters who experience rape, so I will focus instead on three specific moments in the television adaptation that have incited significant controversy: the rape scenes of Daenerys, Sansa, and Cersei. All three scenes were altered from Martin's source text, and so they benefit from an analysis that considers the show and books "as being in a dialogic relationship, together creating a storyworld in which the reading of one might inform the watching of the other and vice versa" (Larsson, 2016:21). When we examine the three adapted scenes and how they portray sexual violence in relation to the books, we see how Martin's text uses rape as a tool to subvert the standard fantasy as 'Disneyland' trope, but also how those scenes portrayal of rape struggle and ultimately fail to break free from standard rape myths that downplay male sexual violence and the agency of its survivors.

Rape Culture

From prime time to cable, from pulp novels and comic books to literary fiction, sexual violence has a long history in western media, and has been used as a narrative tool from the Rape of Lucretia, (the myth detailing the founding of the Roman Republic) to Red Sonja, (the popular pulp character and fantasy trope originator whose rape results in her empowerment). Sarah Projansky argues that depictions of rape are pervasive in American culture, "embedded in all of its complex media forms, entrenched in the landscape of visual imagery" (Projansky, 2001:2). Tanya Horeck expresses a similar notion when she talks about public rape and how the literary, media, and filmic images of rape are sites of collective identification (Horeck, 2004:9). Critical examination of popular media, then, is paramount, as is an interrogation into why and how *GoT*, like its source text, makes a concerted effort to establish its universe as a landscape of sexual threat. Some, like Martin, may argue the case of historical accuracy. As referenced above, Martin claims that his constructed societies, based as they are on the Middle Ages, contain rape because they subscribe to a higher degree of realism than more traditional fantasy fare. But whether a fantasy narrative must include rape and torture to be acceptable to current popular culture consumers, the audience's experience of a rape narrative, particularly onscreen, cannot be dismissed. "Television provides us with texts of the here and now, texts that emanate from the ideological center of society" (Moorti, 2002:18). Rape's very presence on our television screens and in our fiction requires us to examine its purpose and its effects. As Projansky states: "The pervasiveness of representations of rape naturalises rape's place in our everyday world, not only as real physical events but also as part of our fantasies, fears, desires, and consumptive practices." (Projansky, 2001:3). According to feminist scholars then, scenes of rape do not exist in isolation, in-and-of-themselves. Rather, scenes of individual rape are part of a larger system of cultural conceptions of gender and sexuality, both within and outside of the text, often existing within a culture where rape is naturalised, normalised, and trivialised: in other words, a rape culture. As defined by Projansky (9), rape culture, is:

> *a culture in which sexual violence is a normalised phenomenon, in which male-dominant environments ... encourage and sometimes depend on violence against women, in which the male gaze and women as objects-to-be-looked-at contribute to a culture that accepts rape, and in which rape is one experience along a continuum of sexual violence that women confront on a daily basis.*

The result of a society steeped in a rape culture is the proliferation of a variety of myths or tropes, many of which have the troubling tendency to define how sexual violence is reported, understood and communicated from news reports to popular television to everyday assumptions. In the context of how rape culture affects *GoT* and our consumption of its narrative, I would like to highlight and paraphrase some of the myths that Sujata Moorti, in her study on gender and race, lists as perpetrating rape culture (Moorti, 2002:49):

- Rapists are insane; they exist on the fringes of society; they are the Other
- Rape is natural behaviour because men are always-already wanting sex, and women's sexual needs are simply not as urgent
- Women secretly want to be raped
- Women mean "yes" even when they say "no"
- Women will provoke rape, thus only "bad girls" are raped

To these I would add the trend in rape narratives, both in news reports and fiction, to privilege the perpetrator's story and character over the victim's. Equally as troubling is the standard technique of using a woman's rape to propel a male character's story, all of which results in an objectifying, a silencing, and even an erasure of the survivor. The manner in which rape survivors are portrayed in *GoT*, particularly when informed by knowledge of the source text, offers a troubling case study for rape culture's prevalence in popular media.

Daenerys

In its very first episode, "Winter is Coming" (2001), *GoT* established itself as not quite a slavish follower of its source text when it altered the (arguably) consensual sex scene between Daenerys and her new husband, Khal Drogo. The alteration shifted the scene from one of implied rape, (given how Daenerys exercised very little agency in the context of the marriage in the first place), into one of explicit marital rape that, in its overt brutality, established the fantasy world of *GoT* as an environment where the threat of violence is ever-present, and princesses do not achieve happy endings through marriage[1]. Though Drogo shows care and consideration in the book as he attempts to elicit consent from Daenerys in their initial sexual encounter, both the book and the adaptation, (in the following episodes), present Daenerys as a victim of ongoing marital rape:

> *Even the nights brought no relief. Khal Drogo ignored her when they rode, even as he had ignored her during their wedding, and spent his evenings drinking with his warriors and bloodriders, racing his prize horses, watching women dance and men die. Dany had no place in these parts of his life. ... Yet every night, some time before the dawn, Drogo would come to her tent and wake her in the dark, to*

---

[1]. The overturning of expectations here is cemented further in the following scene, where the boy character Bran, with whom the reader/viewer has been led to believe will correspond to general fantasy tropes of the boy-hero, is summarily thrown out of a window to his seeming death.

ride her as relentlessly as he rode his stallion. He always took her from behind, Dothraki fashion, for which Dany was grateful; that way her lord husband could not see the tears that wet her face, and she could use her pillow to muffle her cries of pain. When he was done, he would close his eyes and begin to snore softly and Dany would lie beside him, her body bruised and sore, hurting too much for sleep (Martin, 1996:191-192).

The adaptation, however, in its decision to establish their marriage through a rape scene, emphasises Daenerys's victim status and is unrestrained in its visualisation of a culture based around violence and sex. During their wedding, the camera focus alternates between Daenerys's horrified reactions and Khal Drogo's approval as they witness violent couplings of dubious consent, and the vicious combat between two men that ends in the disembowelment and throat-cutting of the loser, with the winner taking a woman from behind. Daenerys, along with the reader/viewer, is assured that all these events are appropriate to Dothraki weddings, as "a wedding without at least three deaths is deemed a dull affair" (Martin, 1996:85). Daenerys faces the wedding and the task of making Khal Drogo 'happy', (as her brother orders her), with the deportment of one facing a death sentence. When husband and wife are alone, the camera concentrates on Daenerys's tearful face as the Khal undresses her. She attempts to cover herself, but he forces her hands away, and proceeds to bend her over in the animalistic Dothraki fashion previously established during the wedding celebration. The *mise-en-scene* also draws the eye to the contrasting features of the two characters, with the tiny Emilia Clarke almost fetishised in her whiteness and petite size against Jason Momoa's larger form. He literally looms over her. In its quest to emphasise the helplessness and victimisation of the heroine the scene constructs Khal Drogo as a hulking, barbaric Other – thus subscribing to a feature of rape culture discourse that characterises rapists as monstrous and insane. Khal Drogo, however, because he is a person of colour and the leader of a culture we have seen to be barbaric and exotic from the traditional western perspective, also corresponds to another dangerous feature of this "Rapist as Other" trope: the rapist as a dangerous foreigner, a figure used in colonial discourses to justify destructive and racist stereotypes, because of their danger to white women. Operating as they do in politics to popular culture, "rape narratives help structure social understandings of complex phenomena such as gender, race, class, and nation" (Projansky, 2001:7). Within the context of American colonial history, rape, and its association with race, occupies a problematic position. Antonia Castaneda, (1993 quoted in Projansky, 2001:5) argues that "in the eighteenth century U.S. Colonists told *narratives* about Native American men raping white women to justify white male armed violence against Native Americans, while simultaneously using *physical* rape of Native American women as a tool of war against Native Americans and in the name of cultural and national development." Rape is a tool of colonial oppression; a means to label a culture as 'Other': both 'lesser' and dangerous. Thus, in Martin's depiction of Dothraki culture, foregrounded in HBO's alteration to present Daenerys's and Drogo's first coupling as one of rape, the attempt to highlight the heroine's suffering and underdog status plays into these stereotypes of rape and race. And though Drogo later comes to love and respect his wife, their relationship is certainly the exception. The Dothraki generally treat rape as a matter of course, with it being the right of the man to take any woman he wants when he achieves victory (Martin, 1996:557). And though Daenerys does find empowerment through her cultural integration with the Dothraki, and her experience of rape is presented through her perspective, with her pain and debasement as the focus, the Stockholm Syndrome quality of her marriage problematises the empowerment angle, and is only partially resolved with Drogo's death. The binary between source text and adaptation collapses when we read/view Daenerys's experiences in her marriage, and the controversial wedding-night scene foregrounds both the dangerous stereotype of 'Rapist as Other', and the problematic nature of their relationship, where true consent was never an option, and the story becomes one of the victim falling in love with her rapist.

Sansa and Theon

Another character whose experience with sexual abuse the HBO adaptation chose to augment for multiple purposes is Sansa Stark. In both texts, Sansa is the victim of incredible cruelty at the hands of Joffrey and his minions, but after Littlefinger 'rescues' her from Joffrey, and then from her aunt, the texts diverge. With Sansa's narrative cut off in *A Feast for Crows* (Martin, 2005), Benioff and Weiss chose to intertwine Sansa's arc with Theon's, and they bring her to Winterfell as Ramsay Bolton's unwilling bride. In a scene that provoked an intense online reaction from numerous critics, Sansa becomes the victim of marital rape at the hands of one of the most monstrous figures in Westeros. Unlike Drogo, to whom the viewer/reader is introduced in the same scene as the rape, Ramsay's reputation as a violent, insane monster has been thoroughly established through reports of past actions, (such as his forcing Lady Hornwood into a marriage and then abandoning her in a tower to chew her own fingers in a state of starvation), and through Theon's experience of intense physical and psychological torture at his hands. Theon regales us with tales of how Ramsay likes to hunt women, a further conflation of sex and violence: he "catches them he rapes them, flays them, feeds their corpses to his dogs, or brings their skins back to the Dreadfort" (391). Ramsay's insanity is, like other male characters in the narrative, raised to a level of monstrosity that we cannot imagine encountering someone like him in daily life. The HBO audience is, therefore, understandably nervous at Littlefinger's political maneuverings that bring the teenage Sansa into contact with Ramsay, with the prospect of a wedding night not likely to end well.

Bryan Cogman and Jeremy Podeswa, the writer and director of the episode "Unbowed, Unbent, Unbroken" (2015), take care to avoid titillating viewers[2], with Sansa – unlike Daenerys – remaining fully clothed throughout the duration, and with intimate close-ups on Sophie Turner's

---

2. HBO's use of titillation through the pervasiveness of naked female bodies is both pervasive and troubling in its objectifying effect on women, particularly those like Ros whose very purpose as a character is incorporated into her naked body. However, such an examination is, unfortunately, outside the scope of this paper.

face emphasising her trauma. The focus then switches, however, to Theon/Reek, played by Alfie Allen, who is watching from the doorway. The camera slowly zooms in to a close-up of Allen's pained face as he is forced to watch. The director's choice to place the focus on Theon thus parallels Theon's violation with Sansa's, and even privileges Theon's pain as the episode fades to black with his tearful, grimacing face as the viewer's final impression. The following episodes attempt to place Sansa in a rape-revenge narrative, with her progression from despair and suicide contemplation to her escape and desire to wage battle against the Boltons, but though we may find satisfaction in the effort to construct her as a 'Red Sonja', a fantasy trope of a woman who finds empowerment through her rape, the question becomes whether the rape was necessary in the first place. Indeed, her long exposure to the court intrigues at King's Landing, her practice with hiding her feelings behind a shield of courtesy, her continuous suffering at the hands of the Lannisters, the loss of all her family, and her tutelage under Littlefinger are all motivations enough to imagine her capable and willing to escape to her last remaining ally, Jon Snow, and help incite a northern revolt against the Bolton rule, as is depicted in the sixth season. Theon/Reek, on the other hand, absolutely required a significant impetus to shock him out of his traumatised acceptance of the Reek identity. The importance of the rape, then, is especially relevant to Theon's development, in both screen and print. Though strikingly different from the HBO adaptation, *A Dance with Dragons* (Martin, 2011) uses a similar technique of foregrounding Theon's suffering. The reader perceives Ramsay Bolton's wedding night through

Theon's perspective, and the victim is not a character whose inner life has been carefully crafted and whose development we have followed through thousands of pages, but rather the easily forgotten Jeyne Poole, friend and companion to Sansa Stark. As a stand-in for Arya, Jeyne is the means by which the Boltons wish to gain legitimate control over the North, and though her suffering is undoubtedly acute, the reader only perceives her through Theon/Reek's eyes. Like so many of the other rape victims in the narrative who lack a point-of-view, Jeyne is reduced to victim status, her own subjective experience of trauma condensed to a moment of disbelief and tears that evokes horror in her would-be rescuers: "No. This is some trick. It's him, it's my ... my lord, my sweet lord, he sent you, this is just some test to make sure that I love him. ..."' A tear ran down her cheek. 'Tell him, you tell him. I'll do what he wants ... whatever he wants ... [...] ... he doesn't need to cut my feet off, I won't try to run away'" (Martin, 2005:683).

Indeed, Jeyne's (or Sansa's) suffering as a means to snap Theon out of his abused, slave-like mentality is the symptom of a much larger trend in the narrative that is a reflection of the comic book trope 'Women in Refrigerators'. Coined by Gail Simone in response to Green Lantern's girlfriend's murder – and subsequent stuffing in a fridge, the term identifies the standard trope in popular fiction where a female character is killed, tortured, or otherwise put in danger, often by the hero's nemesis, thus providing the hero an emotional stake in the villain's defeat (Asselin, 2014). The 'Women in Refrigerators' trope relegates the woman's role to a narrative device. Both the books and the television adaptation contain many variations on the 'WiR' trope, as rape serves to establish both villainy and sympathy for a male character. In his anti-Disneyland universe, where there are no real heroes, only misfits and underdogs who sport various shades of moral greyness, rape functions as the moral event horizon, the one-step-too-far that a sympathetic protagonist will react against with horror, and never commit. Gregor Clegane, firmly established as a villain through both physical monstrosity and pure viciousness against his opponents in the tourneys, is rendered monstrous through the history we learn from Eddard Stark and Tywin Lannister, who, antagonist mastermind that he is, still baulks at Clegane's rape and murder of Elia Targaryen. "They said he had raped the princess with her son's blood and brains still on his hands" (Martin, 1999:209). Elia's rape and murder provide motivation for Dorne and the entire Martell clan. Lyanna Stark's alleged rape and subsequent death provide much of the emotional depth to Robert Baratheon and reasoning behind his hatred and rebellion against the Targaryen family. Victarion Greyjoy's character development also benefits from a similar rape narrative, when we learn that his brother raped his beloved wife and Victarion was, (in his own mind), forced to kill her (Martin, 2005:420). Tyrion Lannister is the primary beneficiary of the 'fridging' technique, as his history with Tysha is frequently cited throughout the books to provide motivation, explanation and justification for Tyrion's attitude toward women and toward his family.[3] Theon's case, then, is not

---

3. Tyrion Lannister is a complicated figure whose history with women and rape would lend itself well to a comprehensive study on this most popular of characters in Martin's oeuvre. In the interest of space, however, I cannot properly discuss Tyrion's problematic relation to rape culture, as

an isolated incident: male character development has been based around the violation of 'their' women's bodies since before the narrative even begins.

Jaime and Cersei

Martin carefully uses rape and male attitudes toward the act to position problematic characters against those marked as particularly monstrous, thus making said characters more sympathetic. It's a technique he employs to great effect with a character central to the last case study: Jaime Lannister. Jaime begins the series as a firmly established villain, (having thrown Bran out a window), and transitions to an underdog anti-hero figure in his own POV chapters in *A Storm of Swords* (Martin, 2000) through his adventures with Brienne, and by the time of *A Dance with Dragons* is a complex character who, though on the 'wrong' side, the reader (and viewer) can't help but root for as he seeks redemption. In a 2014 interview with *Rolling Stone*'s Mikal Gilmore, Martin explained his fascination with redemption and forgiveness: "One of the things I wanted to explore with Jaime, and with so many of the characters, is the whole issue of redemption. When can we be redeemed? Is redemption even possible? I don't have an answer. But when do we forgive people? … […] … How many good acts make up for a bad act?" The reader/viewer first comes to view Jaime in a more favourable light when he shares the story behind his 'kingslaying', but the character's redemption

---

he does not have a direct bearing on the adapted scenes. Indeed, like Debra Ferreday's careful study of Jaime Lannister, Tyrion Lannister is certainly overdue for a proper study.

and the audience's sympathy is cemented through his rescue of Brienne from the Bloody Mummers. Jaime even empathises with Brienne's situation, and through his own experience with trauma he both understands and advises her on how to cope with the impending rape and torture (Martin, 2000:242, 344). Brienne herself, though a fully-formed character in her own right whose experience with male disrespect reaches back long before Jaime, is placed in a position of powerlessness, one commonly associated with her gender, thus providing Jaime with an opportunity to display a traditional type of heroism, the rescuing of the damsel in distress, as motivation and proof of his character development. With their friendship firmly entrenched and his respect for Brienne a positive influence, Jaime, who would not hesitate to push a child out a window two books previously, but also would not allow a woman, his captor though she may be, fall victim to rape and torture, seemed on the path to unexpected redemption and in full possession of the audience's sympathy. Through a careful strategy of friendship born from reluctant acceptance and a dramatic rescue, Martin subverts audience expectation for Jaime-as-villain, and instead establishes him as a popular anti-hero to rival Tyrion.

The final rape scene to consider, adapted from *A Storm of Swords* into the episode "Breaker of Chains" (2014), ruptures Jaime's redemption arc even as it also subverts the previously established 'Rapist as Monster' trope (though it fails to escape others). When Jaime forces Cersei into sex by the tomb of their deceased son, audience expectations are completely overturned; after all, even in a universe populated with morally grey anti-heroes, the underdog on a path to redemption or success is one trope we have, heretofore, relied upon. The likeability of the perpetrator, his adherence to a positive narrative type (villain redeemed into anti-hero), creates reluctance to interpret the act as rape, and even the showrunners and director expressed contradictory opinions on the topic. Alex Graves, the director, explicitly stated in a 2014 interview with Uproxx's Alan Sepinwall: "Well, it becomes consensual by the end, because anything for them ultimately results in a turn-on, especially a power struggle." But the scene, with Cersei's repeated calls for Jaime to "stop" and Jaime's reply "I don't care" (2014), confirms a definition of rape when considered the act of engaging in sex without the partner's explicit consent. Blogs and articles debated the appropriateness of 'HBO Jaime's' action, declaring it to be "the most screwed up sex scene ever broadcast on television" (Stern, 2014), and completely out of character for Jaime (Romano, 2014). Debra Ferreday, in her comprehensive article about this scene and the fandom's reaction, entrenched as it is in current rape culture, used the term 'rupture' to describe a moment like this, where the expected outcome is subverted, and a male's future is spoiled (2015:33-34).[4] A glance at Jaime's character in the books, however, problematises fan construction of Jaime as a redeemed figure for whom rape would be completely unacceptable. Jaime's character is based around the juxtaposition of violence and sex; he sees violence as romance, and sex (with Cersei) as a struggle. In

---

4. Ferreday's article also interrogates the fan reaction in the context of current rape culture, where the public's reaction to rape, particularly on college campuses, is often one of regret over the accused male perpetrator's spoiled future.

his fight with Brienne, his blood sings as "the swords kissed and sprang apart and kissed again" (Martin, 2000:238) In the novel's version of the HBO scene, Jaime and Cersei do engage in sex, but, while it is certainly depicted as a struggle that results in a 'turn-on', it is difficult to gauge the consensual quality because the scene is from Jaime's perspective, and Jaime is overcome with his own desires. The moment begins with him comforting her, but "there was no tenderness in the kiss he returned to her" (700), and she protests, albeit weakly, at how the septons might catch them while pounding on his chest with "feeble fists" (ibid) while he pushes and tears at her legs and clothes. As the aggressor in both versions, Jaime, (and Cersei's seemingly token protests), subscribes to the rape myth trope that men's sexual needs are simply more urgent, and their aggression thus naturalised. Jorah Mormont, in an argument Jaime or Robert Baratheon or any of the other men defined by violent actions would support, defends the uncontrollable urges of men when he says, describing the aftermath of battle: "More women were raped than you can count. There is a savage beast in every man, and when you hand that man a sword ... and send him forth to war, the beast stirs" (271). The imbalance in the scene and fan discourse thus simultaneously privileges Jaime while ignoring, and thus silencing and disempowering, Cersei.

The result of all this ambiguity and the privileging of Jaime is the erasure of Cersei's perspective on the experience. Indeed, Graves's comment plays into the dangerous rape culture myth that "women mean 'yes' even when they say 'no'" (Moorti, 2002:49). The narrative explicitly expresses support for the trope in Cersei's character itself. The exotic

Lady Taena describes her relationship with her husband: "A hundred times I told him no, and he said yes … […] … until finally I was saying yes as well" (Martin, 2000:254), and Cersei thinks of Jaime with a smile. The establishing of their relationship as one that equates sex with struggle, and, of course, the taboo nature of that relationship in the first place, also would serve to render Cersei's protestations, should she ever voice them, as moot. Ripping gowns and turning blows to kisses is the established trend among the two (392). Cersei is, in rape culture myth, a 'bad girl' – part of the myth that "women invite rape and provoke their rapists" (Moorti, 2002:49). When the narrative does allow her a moment of pathos, as she thinks of how "Robert would use her when the drink was in him" (Martin, 2005:481), it is during a moment of Cersei using another for sex. In fact, Cersei is one of two female characters who voices her own trauma, but, through her antagonistic position against most of the protagonists to which the audience is sympathetic, like Ned Stark and Tyrion, she is also established as a villain, or at least an antagonist, of the piece.[5] Of course Cersei's actions do not delegitimize her experience or trauma, but in

---

5. The second character who narrates her own trauma is Mirri Maaz Duur. A victim of repeated rapes from the Dothraki, Duur is a complex figure who evokes both sympathy and resentment from the reader, much like Cersei. She is uncompromising and realistic in her confrontation with the naïve Daenerys of the first book regarding just how much Daenerys really 'saved' her from her fate; but she is also the destroyer of Daenerys's hopes and dreams in her destructive magic against Khal Drogo and Daenerys's unborn son. But while the 'villain' status of Cersei and Duur is complicated, the lack of other female survivor narration of sexual violation foregrounds the two textual examples we have, as well as their limitations.

the carefully crafted narrative that Martin and others have constructed, the position of Cersei as a villainess who uses sex for power and whose consensual incest is altered into an incestuous rape that is never revisited in either book or show represents a troubling tendency to flatten the female experience. Though the HBO adaptation somewhat combats this with Lena Headey's strong performance, Martin spends thousands of pages constructing Cersei as a vicious, though somewhat inept, antagonist, to whom the reader is not sympathetically disposed. Jaime's more traditionally likeable character, his narrative of the rape, is privileged, both through this technique and through the imbalance in their point-of-view, and Cersei's, as a result, is erased.

When narratives employ and subscribe to rape myths, and privilege the male narrative over that of the survivor's, the result is a silencing and an objectifying of the female, her body and her experience. Instead of a subject producing her own meaning, she becomes an object on which men, writers and characters, project their own meanings. Projansky describes how "rape bolsters male power, and the bodies of raped women function as symbols of violent communication between men" (Projansky, 2001:42). We see this with Sansa, whose marriage and rape acts in-text as a motivation for Theon to overcome his trauma and, within the context of popular tropes from classic, male-driven fantasy, constructs her character as a 'Red Sonja' figure in a rape-revenge style narrative. We see this with Cersei, whose rape is a moment of rupture for Jaime's character, and is not even interpreted as rape by the episode's director. But these case studies are merely primary examples of a 'rape as window-dressing' type approach that Martin frequently employs in his quest to subvert fantasy tropes and establish a landscape of perpetual threat. Victims, unprotected from objectification because of their lack of a voice, either introspectively through a point-of-view chapter or the opportunity to vocalise the trauma, populate the narrative in droves. Tysha, Lyanna Stark and Elia Targaryen are examples whose experiences are translated through male voices, their rapes and deaths inscribed with meaning by the men who were affected, both publicly and privately, from their rapes. Lollys Stokeworth is another example, a minor noblewoman whose gang rape is the symbol for the disintegration of civil order in King's Landing under Joffrey's reign in *A Clash of Kings* (Martin, 1999). Her character's trauma is only addressed through comments and reactions of other characters, like Sansa and Tyrion's uncomfortable pity, and explicit contempt and disgust from Shae and Cersei. Her trauma, in fact, seems to render her incapable of speech, a weeping and sleeping and eating automaton. Shae complains: "Sleep's all she ever wants to do, the great cow. She sleeps and she eats. Sometimes she falls asleep while she's eating" (Martin, 2000:587). Others, like pretty Pia, are passed between dominant male groups much like the castles they conquer. And though she is eventually rescued, the symbolism of silencing behind Gregor Clegane's smashing of her mouth in punishment for speaking out of turn is hard to deny (Martin, 2005:404). Some are not even allowed even that much voice. Gregor Clegane's monstrosity is frequently emphasised in moments of passing reference to female rape victims. Ned Stark sends Beric Dondarrion to execute Clegane after "a young girl in a bloody dress" supplicates herself before Ned but finds herself incapable of voicing what was done to her: "'They killed my mother ... [...] ... and they ... they ...' Her voice trailed off, as if she had forgotten what she was going to say" (Martin, 1996:387-388). Later, Arya observes how one girl in Harrenhal, "prettier than the others, was made to go with four or five different men every night, until finally she hit one with a rock. Ser Gregor made everyone watch while he took off her head with a sweep of his ... greatsword" (Martin, 1999:314). The most horrifying example, however, occurs in the next Arya chapter, when she overhears Chiswyck describe, in lurid detail, the rape of a brewer's thirteen-year-old daughter (349-350). Named only once in passing as Layna, the girl's experience is related in a second-hand narration that describes how the girl was viciously raped, first by Clegane and then by all of his men in turn, in punishment for her father's defence of her virtue. The tale is uncompromising and brutal and serves three purposes: to emphasise Gregor Clegane's monstrosity, (in case we have forgotten); to establish Chiswyck as particularly repulsive; and to provide Arya with enough motivation to murder the latter. The rape, both in its act and in its telling, has nothing to do with the victim, and the girl is never mentioned again. These interchangeable women become collateral damage not only to Clegane and his Bloody Mummers, but also to the narrative technique of establishing monstrosity and danger at the expense of individual female bodies. Their experience is flattened and silenced, much like Cersei's with Jaime; their purpose and meaning expressed only through their violation, similar to the 'fridging' moment of Sansa. The altered rape scenes in the HBO adaptation are, therefore, not anomalies, but rather canaries in the coal mine that alert the audience to the noxious fumes of rape culture tropes constructing the landscape of Westeros and informing our understanding of its narratives.

Conclusion

The consequence of rape as a tool utilised to subvert the sanitised, fairytale-like fantasy Martin and HBO are writing against, is a general disempowering of the female survivors and victims. Though some characters, particularly Daenerys[6], but even Cersei in relation to Robert's marital abuse, transcend their 'victim' status to become 'survivors' through their comparatively privileged position as point-of-view narrators, the vast majority of characters are relegated to the status of victim or object, their personal voices erased as their violated bodies signify power exchanges between men. The multitude of examples illustrates how rape, in Martin's Westeros, is a constant threat from men both monstrous and sympathetic. The effect on the female characters, however, is damaging: "In fantasy worlds, as in reality, subversion is often achieved at the expense of the objectification and violation of the female and raced body" (Ferreday, 2015:28). In their quest to subvert the general 'Disneyland' sentiment inherent to medieval settings, Martin, and HBO's Benioff and Weiss, employ

---

6. Daenerys is a complicated case in relation to rape culture myths, because while she is one of the few women of the narrative who is both healthily empowered and sexual, her marriage and sexual encounters with Khal Drogo perpetuate stereotypes of the racist Other, a Beauty and the Beast narrative where the victim falls in love with her rapist, and a general lack of interrogating marital rape as an issue.

rape myths that objectify and disempower the female body and experience. Feminist critique proves, once again, that though popular fantasy is capable of accommodating both dragons and ice zombies, women in fantasy narratives, even the strong ones, continue to fall victim to narratives that privilege the male experience, reflecting the current rape culture that continues to dominate public discourse around women and their sexual experiences.

Bibliography

Asselin, J., 2014. *Gail Simone: The Comic Alliance Interview, Part One – Batgirl, Birds of Prey, and Women in Refrigerators*. [online] Available at: <http://comicsalliance.com/gail-simone-the-comics-alliance-interview-part-one-batgirl-birds-of-prey-and-women-in-refrigerators/> [Accessed 4 December 2016].

Breaker of Chains, 2014. Game of Thrones, series 4 episode 3. [TV programme]. HBO, 20 April 2014.

Ferreday, D., 2015. Game of Thrones, Rape Culture And Feminist Fandom. *Australian Feminist Studies* 30(83): 21-36.

Gilmore, M., 2014. *George R.R. Martin: The Rolling Stone Interview*. [online] Available at: <http://www.rollingstone.com/tv/news/george-r-r-martin-the-rolling stone-interview-20140423> [Accessed 29 December 2016]

Hibberd, J., 2015. *George R.R. Martin Explains Why There's Violence Against Women on 'Game of Thrones'*. [online] Available at: <http://ew.com/article/2015/06/03/george-rr-martin-thrones-violence-women/> [Accessed 11 January 2017].

Horeck, T., 2004. *Public Rape*. London: Routledge.

Hudson, L., 2014. *That Game of Thrones Scene Wasn't a 'Turn-On,' It Was Rape.* [online] Available at: <http://www.wired.com/2014/04/game-of-thrones-rape/> [Accessed 15 January 2017].

Larsson, M., 2016. Adapting Sex: Cultural Conceptions of Sexuality in Words and Images. In A. Gjelsvik and R. Schubart, eds. 2016. *Women of Ice and Fire: Gender, Game of Thrones, and Multiple Media Engagements*. New York: Bloomsbury. 17-38.

Martin, George R.R., 1996. *A Game of Thrones*. New York: Bantam Books.

Martin, George R.R., 1999. *A Clash of Kings*. New York: Bantam Books.

Martin, George R.R., 2000. *A Storm of Swords*. New York: Bantam Books.

Martin, George R.R., 2005. *A Feast for Crows*. New York: Bantam

Books.

Martin, George R.R., 2011. *A Dance with Dragons*. New York: Bantam Books.

Moorti, S., 2002. *Color of Rape*. Albany: State University of New York Press.

Pappas, S., 2014. *How Real is the 'Game of Thrones' Medieval World?* [online] Available at: <http://www.livescience.com/44599-medieval-reality-game-of-thrones.html> [Accessed 20 January 2017].

Peterson, D., 2015. The Languages of Ice and Fire. In J. Battis. and S. Johnston, ed. 2015. *Mastering the Game of Thrones: Essays on George R.R. Martin's A Song of Ice and Fire*. Jefferson: McFarland & Company, Inc. 15-34.

Projansky, S., 2001. *Watching Rape*. New York: New York University Press.

Romano, A., 2014. *Why We Should Pretend the 'Game of Thrones' Rape Scene Never Happened.* [online] Available at: <http://www.thedailybeast.com/articles/2014/05/04/why-we-should-pretend-the-game-of-thrones-rape-scene-never-happened.html> [Accessed 20 February 2017].

Sepinwall, A., 2014. *Review: 'Game of Thrones' – 'Breaker of Chains'*. [online] Available at: <http://uproxx.com/sepinwall/review-game-of-thrones-breaker-of-chains-uncle-deadly/> [Accessed 21 February 2017].

Tolkien, J.R.R., 1954. The Lord of the Rings. London: George Allen and Unwin.

Unbowed, Unbent, Unbroken, 2015. Game of Thrones, series 6, episode 2. [TV programme]. HBO, 15 May 2015.

Winter is Coming, 2011. Game of Thrones, series 1, episode 1. [TV programme]. HBO, 17 April 2017.

The Magical Way Forward? - Recent Changes in Gender Representation in *'Magic: The Gathering'* Card Game

By Rostislav Kůrka

This paper focuses on the portrayal of gender in the story of "Magic: The Gathering" card game. Recently, growing focus on the story itself has been accompanied by a notable shift in the way characters of different genders have been represented. Using particular cases from Magic's recent story blocks, the aim of this paper is to pinpoint and evaluate the trends in this development, both quantitative (in terms of female/male/non-binary ratio of characters appearing in the story) and qualitative (the roles these characters take on). Roles of characters belonging to sexual orientation minorities are also discussed.

In the last few years, a notable shift has occurred in the story and game of *Magic: The Gathering*. This popular fantasy card game, one of the most popular in the world, has been around since 1993 and has always been accompanied by an ongoing narrative. In 2014 its creators decided to really emphasise the storyline aspect. *Magic* thus entered its new, "story-driven" era. As stated by Doug Beyer, senior creative designer of *Magic*:

> *Around the time of Tarkir block, we decided to stop hiding the main storyline in for-sale products, to weave it into the card set itself, and to share it freely on the web. Since then, readership has exploded, player awareness of the events of the story is at an*

all-time high, and Magic as a whole feels like it's not just decorated with but driven by story." (Beyer 2016)

At the same time, another aspect seems to be working hand-in-hand with this development: *Magic* is changing the way it portrays and represents characters in terms of gender. This concerns both their depiction on cards and the way they are handled in the story. In this article, I have focused mainly on the storyline part to avoid branching out too much;[1] however, the impact of the story shift on the portrayal of characters on cards shall also be briefly mentioned.

The centre of my interest is the most recent developments, especially since the release of the *Khans of Tarkir* expansion (2014), up to the last expansion set of 2016, *Kaladesh*. That covers the era from the moment when the main narrative, originally reserved for paper and later e-novels, was transferred into the *Uncharted Realms* column (later renamed *Magic Story*) on Wizards of the Coast's official website.

Quantitative Representation

The first remarkable trend in *Magic*'s recent development is the quantitative difference in the amount of male and

---

[1]. A visual aspect of Magic in relation to gender would deserve its own study, and probably more than one. There is not, to my knowledge, an up-to-date research on the topic. A fairly recent and very good study, covering the time just before the "story shift", is Fornazari&Macedo (2016).

female characters that appear in the story (and game). This concerns both major and minor characters.

As part of the shift in storytelling, the authors have established a "central cast" by selecting five pre-existing characters to keep as recurring protagonists. Each of these characters represents one of the five colours of *Magic*.[2] They are Gideon Jura (male hieromancer,[3] white), Nissa Revane (female elf animist, green), Jace Beleren (male telepath, blue), Chandra Nalaar (female pyromancer, red) and Liliana Vess (female necromancer, black). All of them are Planeswalkers, i.e. wizards capable of travelling between the multitudes of worlds that make up the *Magic* universe. Following the events of the "Battle for Zendikar" story block (released October 2015-January 2016), the main cast have formed "the Gatewatch" - a group not unlike the superhero teams we are familiar with from comics such as *X-Men* or *The Avengers*. Their purpose is to protect the Multiverse from threats that the inhabitants of individual worlds cannot face alone. Each of the heroes has their own motivation for joining the Gatewatch.

The composition of the central cast is already remarkable in terms of its ratio of male and female characters. As it stands, there are three female (Nissa, Chandra, Liliana) and two male characters (Gideon, Jace). Currently, the majority

---

2. The game mechanics operate with five colours of magic and cards belong to one or more colours (white, blue, black, red, green). Each colour has its own strengths, weaknesses and flavour. For example, red is the colour of fire, destruction (but also creativity), passion and emotions (both positive and negative). Blue is the colour of intellect, rationality and progress.

3. I.e. a mage specialised in "law magic" used to prevent others from attacking.

of "super-teams" in mainstream fantasy or sci-fi comics, films and TV shows tend to be either 50-50 or leaning towards a majority of male characters.[4] In a team of heroes, the female member is often treated as if this was her primary defining characteristic: thus a team might feature, for example, a warrior, a mage, a ranger and a female. Having more characters of the same gender by default creates pressure on the author to make each of them different. *Magic*'s central cast, therefore, provides an alternative to the prevalent lack of variety in female character roles. As a classic of its genre (having been around for over twenty years), it shows that things need not always be forced according to a predetermined scheme.

A similar approach can be observed with regards to secondary characters, not just the central cast. A remarkable instance of this was the *Khans of Tarkir* expansion (released September 2014). Its story preceded the establishment of the recurring cast, and therefore its focus was on characters closely tied to the world it was set in. Tarkir was a world once inhabited by dragons, now ruled by five khans – the leaders of five warrior-clans, who long ago had hunted the dragons into extinction. Of the titular characters, three were female and two male.[5]

---

4. Of similar "super-teams" featured in some major recent sci-fi films, both *Guardians of the Galaxy* (2014) and *Avengers: Age of Ultron* (2015) have several male characters and one "token" female among the central cast. The *X-Men: Apocalypse* (2016) team have a more balanced ratio, however the men are still essentially in the majority. *Rogue One: A Star Wars Story* (2016) has one female lead character surrounded by male characters.

5. Female Khans (according to their names on their cards): Anafenza, the Foremost; Narset, Enlightened Master; Sidisi, Brood Tyrant. Male

The fact that *Magic*'s creators opted to make the majority of the khans female is perhaps even more remarkable because of its "masculine" setting. War and leadership have not often been traditionally considered to be places for women, and even if "warrior women" are an existing trope in fantasy, they are usually considered exceptional and have to fight their way through the ranks (unless they hail from an "Amazon culture", which is, again, a special environment). Female leaders on Tarkir aren't treated as exceptions to the rule, but are instead on an equal footing with men. Tarkir builds on the imagery of ancient Central Asian nomadic cultures, where most would expect the leader to resemble (male) Genghis Khan. One comparable example of this in recent mainstream fantasy literature would be the Dothraki in George R. R. Martin's *A Song of Ice and Fire* (1996-2011), who are clearly a male-dominated culture (the exiled princess Daenerys, an outsider who becomes their "Khaleesi", is an anomaly) in this mould.

In the second expansion of the Khans of Tarkir block[6], *Fate Reforged*, set in Tarkir's past, the world's history is changed. Ultimately, in *Dragons of Tarkir*, five dragon broods rule the plane instead of the five Khans. This creates a set of fifteen central characters from the world of Tarkir: ten Khans (five in present Tarkir, five in the past) and five Dragonlords (who continue to live from the time of *Fate Reforged* to the present).

Khans: Surrak Dragonclaw; Zurgo Helmsmasher.

6. *Magic*'s expansion sets are released in blocks linked by the same story and setting. *Khans of Tarkir* (September 2014) was the first set of a block which also included *Fate Reforged* (January 2015) and *Dragons of Tarkir* (March 2015).

Fate Reforged reverses the ratio of male and female Khans[7] and the clans that had male leaders in the present have female leaders in the past. This would make the ratio balanced if it weren't for the fact that in the same expansion the dragons (not extinct yet) appear, divided into five broods of which each has its own Dragonlord. Out of these, three Dragonlords are female and two male.[8] In *Dragons of Tarkir*, the same Dragonlords make a comeback.

Both the Khans and the Gatewatch represent a trend which is, even today, still rare among both fantasy and non-fantasy literature and games. Even if nowadays it is much less likely for a book or film to "forget" to include at least a few female characters, there are still not many stories where female characters form the bulk of the protagonists (unless the book or film is specifically aimed at a female audience, dealing with environments where female characters can be expected, etc.). In games (board, computer, even other card games), the situation is mostly similar, if not even less balanced.[9] *Magic*, as the most widely played fantasy card game in the world, proves that to have a central cast where female characters are the majority need not in any way seem strange to the mainstream audience.[10]

---

7. Female Khans in Fate Reforged: Alesha, Who Smiles At Death; Yasova Dragonclaw. Male Khans: Daghatar the Adamant; Shu-Yun, the Silent Tempest; Tasigur, the Golden Fang.

8. Female Dragonlords: Atarka, Dromoka, Kolaghan. Male Dragonlords: Ojutai, Silumgar.

9. See Fornazari&Macedo (2016), who point out that e.g. majority of computer games have a white male protagonist.

10. Especially if those characters are not sexualized. See below.

Female, Male: Non-binary Protagonists Ratio

If we look at all the *Magic* stories published under the new system of storytelling, we can see the trend applying globally. Out of these stories, a slight majority (roughly 56%) had a female protagonist/viewpoint character. Recently, characters that do not ascribe to either of the two genders have also appeared. Most of the protagonists have their own cards in the game, although some appear only in the story.

In the table below, I have listed the stories forming the plot of the last set of 2016, *Kaladesh* (Kreines, 2016d).

Story	Characters appearing as viewpoint characters in the story		
	Male	Female	Non-binary
Homesick	-	Liliana Vess, Chandra Nalaar, Nissa Revane	-
A Time for Innovation	-	Rashmi, Saheeli Rai	-
Torch of Defiance	-	Chandra Nalaar	-
Renegade Prime	-	Pia Nalaar, Liliana Vess	-

Story	Characters appearing as viewpoint characters in the story		
	Male	**Female**	**Non-binary**
Born of Aether	-	-	Yahenni
Bottled Up	-	Nissa Revane	-
Release	Ajani, Nashi	-	-
In this Very Arena	Jace Beleren, Consul Kambal	Nissa Revane, Pia Nalaar, Chandra Nalaar	-
A Grateful Consulate	Dovin Baan	-	-
Total # of protagonists	5	12	1

Prominence of female characters in this story block is even more notable than in the whole sample (even though it is largely influenced by the story's focus on Chandra's reunion with her mother).

The main storyline[11] from *Khans of Tarkir* to *Kaladesh* consists of 85 individual stories. Among those, 45 feature at least one male protagonist (i.e. protagonist addressed in the text as "he"), 48 feature at least one female protagonist (addressed in the text as "she"), and one features a

---
11. Related to "standard" expansions. I opted to leave supplementary products out to avoid broadening the scope too much.

protagonist who is not assigned either of the two genders (addressed in the text as "they"). Nine stories feature both male and female protagonists.

Nameless minor characters that appear in the story cannot be easily quantified in this way, but in their case too, we can speak roughly about a 50-50 distribution between female and male characters. This concerns nameless characters, regardless of their role or profession.

The push for having more female characters now than in the past was also confirmed by *Magic*'s head designer Mark Rosewater (2016b) in relation to the Three, ancient Planeswalkers who, in the plot, play the role of a (failed) forerunner to the Gatewatch. Originally, they were introduced in Zendikar block's story (autumn 2009 - spring 2010) as the vampire Sorin Markov (male), spirit dragon Ugin (male) and the Lithomancer (unknown, because she was only mentioned). Only in *The Lithomancer* story (Kreines 2015a), the latter was named Nahiri and her gender established as female. Before that, while being known only by her epithet, many players perceived her as male, even though "Lithomancer" is a gender-neutral word. Most people would imagine a male figure under a gender-neutral word (such as "smith" or "leader"), unless they expected the "profession" to be primarily associated with the female gender (see e.g. Gastil 1990). Wizards of the Coast left the Lithomancer's identity open for half a decade,[12] and it is possible to imagine that, had the Three been created in 2010, they would have been all male. On the contrary, Rosewater (2016b) recently wrote: "If we had to do it over, Ugin would

---

12. In an article by Beyer (2010), which was the first to summarise the story of the Three, the Lithomancer is mentioned only vaguely.

have been female." It is therefore possible that, had the characters been created today, they might have been two females (Nahiri, Ugin) and one male (Sorin). This would correspond to the attitude Wizards of the Coast adopted in the case of the Gatewatch and lately, in general.

Giving preference to female characters makes sense as conscious opposition to the generic tendency to fill in "undecided" characters as male by default. If the culturally ingrained processes in our minds make writers more likely to subconsciously assign male gender to "blank" characters, one way to counter this obvious imbalance is to consciously give preference to non-male characters (unless there is a plot reason for doing otherwise). The answer to the question "Why would Wizards of the Coast push for a majority of female characters?" is actually not "inclusivity" or "balance". The appropriate answer, in my opinion, is simply *why not*? If we are talking pure numbers, gender doesn't mean anything. It says nothing about the roles male, female or other characters play in the story. Because of that, there is no reason why they should be female, but equally no reason why they should *not* be female.

Qualitative Representation

How are *Magic*'s female characters portrayed, then? If these characters were strongly sexualised, their large numbers would just mean a more varied selection of "poster girls" on the cards. Here is where I believe the story-driven approach of *Magic* plays its part. If the intention is "to weave [the story] into the card set itself" (Beyer 2016), for example, then a card representing a careful, experienced female hunter has to convey those character traits and not a suggestively posed, scantily clad girl. Recent expansions of *Magic*, as opposed to older ones, don't have provocatively posed female characters. We also don't find them wearing revealing clothes for no good reason. Out of the female khans in the *Khans of Tarkir* block, only the Naga Sidisi is wearing "revealing" clothing - she is a serpent. Human female Khans wear either full body armour (Anafenza, Alesha), monk robes (Narset) or furs (Yasova Dragonclaw). There is no attempt to make their outfits "bikini armour" or other such outfits that are commonly used in many fantasy settings, games, book covers, etc. (Fornazari & Macedo 2016). The same applies to other minor characters. Characters who already existed in older sets and previously had revealing outfits tend to now be given much more functional gear befitting their role in the story.[13]

Like many other media, *Magic* and its story have mostly focused on young characters, both in its protagonists and supporting characters, until very recently. The sudden awareness and attempt to introduce more major characters of different ages seems to be one of the observable trends since *Shadows Over Innistrad* (February 2016). It is relevant to our discussion because, from a gender perspective, older women tend to be under-represented because of their presumed lack of sexual attractiveness. Out of six Planeswalkers appearing

---

13. A good example being the vampire leader Drana. On her card, "Drana, Kalastria Bloodchief" from *Rise of the Eldrazi* (2010), she wears a black body suit, showing plenty of cleavage. In *Battle for Zendikar* (2015), she returns as the commander of the vampire forces in the story "Memories of Blood" (Kreines 2015c). On "Drana, Liberator of Malakir", her outfit covers her body as she leads her armies into battle.

on cards in *Shadows Over Innistrad* block, two were middle-aged females: Arlinn Kord, a werewolf "protector mother of the pack", and Tamiyo, a moonfolk scientist. The first remarkable elderly character, artificer Oviya Pashiri, made an appearance in *Kaladesh* and became instrumental to the plot. Chandra Nalaar's mother, the artificer and renegade Pia Nalaar, is central to the story.

Stereotypes Revisited and Broken

The first five members of the Gatewatch were created a long time ago[14] and therefore carry signs of a different approach to character portrayal than those we see in newly created characters. The shift in Wizards of the Coast's take on gender is visible here upon closer inspection. Originally, the "Lorwyn Five" (including Chandra, Jace and Liliana) had been mainly created to represent archetypes associated with their colours (fire mage, mind mage and death mage, respectively), without giving them much personality beyond that. Gideon and Nissa only appeared later but they too conform to certain archetypes ("good knight" and a nature mage).

The cast, at the time of their formation, fits the most basic gender stereotypes: men possess physical strength, moral

---

14. Chandra Nalaar, Jace Beleren and Liliana Vess were part of the so-called "Lorwyn Five", the first five Planeswalkers printed on cards (*Lorwyn* expansion, 2007). Gideon Jura appeared later as a replacement for the original white Planeswalker, Ajani Goldmane, and Nissa Revane appeared as a replacement for green Planeswalker, Garruk Wildspeaker, thus tipping the balance towards a majority of female characters among the central cast.

integrity, bravery and leadership qualities (Gideon) along with rationality, calmness and the ability to solve problems (Jace). Women's remarkable traits are unchecked emotions and chaotic behaviour, which can be potentially destructive (Chandra), "feminine" connection with nature and almost otherworldly beauty (Nissa), and alluring seductiveness combined with inner wickedness (Liliana). All these traits have remained with the characters until present day, but the ongoing story has added and brought other qualities to the front. The most striking example, Liliana Vess, has had her *femme fatale* trope downplayed. By portraying her as a protagonist, she becomes rather the model of a mature woman whose goal is to remain in charge of her own destiny.[15]

On the contrary, newly created characters tend not to fit into the masculine/feminine dichotomy of archetypes. Recent story blocks feature a remarkable amount of female leaders (Khans and Dragonlords of Tarkir; the vampire leader Drana or the allied general Tazri of Zendikar; the knight Thalia or the vampire noble Olivia Voldaren on Innistrad; the renegade leader Pia Nalaar of Kaladesh, intellectual authorities (Tamiyo in *Eldritch Moon*; in *Kaladesh*, the inventor Rashmi, whose inventions will probably have a far-reaching impacts on the whole *Magic* universe), or even women in unusual professions (Kaladesh's best race driver, the dwarven pilot Depala). Each of these characters (except Depala) feature as chief protagonists in at least one story of

---

15. Liliana is actually several hundred years old and owes her powers and her youthful appearance to demonic contracts she has made. Her story is essentially a personal quest to free herself of the demons she's indebted to.

their own.

Female authority in a particular field is accepted in the same way as male authority, and if it is challenged, it is never because of gender. In the *Eldritch Moon* story, Jace Beleren accepts Tamiyo as a more experienced mentor and listens to her. In the *Battle for Zendikar* story block, Tazri replaces Gideon in command of the allied armies of an entire world. The *Magic* story, overall, presents a setting that does not discriminate on the basis of gender. This approach helps to break stereotypes undermining women in leading positions as somehow naturally unfit to be in charge.

What is missing, however, is the opposite trend: male characters appearing in traditionally feminine roles or showing feminine traits. The story, for example, does not tend to feature male characters as homemakers, or as being interested in their appearance or in aesthetics in general. On the contrary, the one recurring case of a male character's outfit being mentioned is Jace's cloak: Jace seems to be wearing the same cloak all the time, submitting to the stereotype that men don't really care about what they wear.

Non-Binary Characters

Questioning the concept of what is masculine/feminine brings us to another appearing trend in the *Magic* story; that is, the emergence of characters who do not belong to either of the two genders or who are not defined by their gender at all.

Once again, it is an example of the influence of the culture we live in on the writers, that most of our literature operates only with characters of the two clearly defined genders: male and female. Even if a particular author does not perceive gender as a fluid concept (or a scale rather than two opposite poles), it is surprising that the binary is so strongly inscribed into our way of thinking that even fantasy, of all genres, does not come up more often with different expressions of this. In fantasy, by definition, everything should be possible and we could expect creatures or monsters with more genders, fewer genders or no genders at all. Regardless, this happens less often than one would expect and the majority of characters, even fantastic creatures, have male and female genders.

Misgendered Characters: A Retcon

Magic's creators have recently made statements regarding the fact that they had "misgendered" genderless characters in the past. This marks the rising awareness of different concepts of gender among *Magic*'s writers and creators. What I consider notable is that Wizards of the Coast believed this to be an important enough matter to bring it up a long time after it had happened.

This issue primarily concerns the silver golem Karn, one of the main characters of the Weatherlight Saga, the first story to be directly referenced on the cards.[16] Karn has always been referred to as "he", even though he is without

---

16. The Weatherlight saga started with Weatherlight (1997) and continued through the Tempest block, the Masques block and ended with the Invasion block (2001). Its main plot was the journey of the flying ship Weatherlight and its crew. As the first story to be simultaneously narrated via novels and through card flavour text, it was the first step and a direct forerunner to the current way of storytelling.

sex and, as a construct, could be expected to be without gender as well. Mark Rosewater, who was also behind the original Weatherlight saga, has repeatedly confirmed Karn as being genderless. In response to fans' confusion with regards to Karn being called "he", Rosewater (2016a) wrote:

> *"Karn has no gender. Others refer to Karn as "he" because Karn looks more male than female. (And Karn was referred to as "he" in the story because back in the mid 90's when Karn was created, the concept of agender wasn't something the general public, including Michael and I, who made the character, was aware of).*
>
> *Karn does not consider himself male or female. Karn doesn't correct others because it just isn't something Karn makes an issue out of. If I understand correctly (and please let me know if I'm wrong), it's about how someone identifies themselves, not how others choose to identify them."*

In Karn's case, the response of *Magic*'s creators seems to be an effort to set right a past misgendering of a major and popular character; a correction of something that should have been done differently in the first place. This correction does not introduce any drastic reversal. Despite being a "retcon", it does not change the way Karn is being addressed, only Karn's self-perception. Mark Rosewater's reaction therefore cannot be attributed only to some kind of attempt to appease the fans, but to his personal recognition that there was something he did not know at the time the story was written. The catalyst, however, was seemingly the interaction with the reader community, which is a direct result of the influx in readership and interest in the story.

Non-Gendered and Transgender Characters

Magic has recently quite visibly tackled the non-binary concept of gender. The first notable character without specified gender was the Planeswalker Ashiok, who appeared as a minor antagonist during the *Theros* block (2013-14), which directly preceded the *Khans of Tarkir* and the shift to a story-driven mode. Medwin (2015) clarified: "Ashiok's gender is canonically defined as an enigma, and I know a lot of people have latched onto Ashiok as an example of a genderqueer/agender character." A more specific example is the Aetherborn from recent *Kaladesh* expansions (autumn 2016). They were introduced as a new race native to Kaladesh, born of the Aether that circulates the world's ecosystem. As such, they do not have gender and refer to themselves by the pronoun "they". The story of *Kaladesh* features two named Aetherborn characters: Yahenni and the crime lord Gonti. Yahenni is the protagonist of the story *Born of Aether*, in which they aid the Gatewatch in locating Chandra's captive mother.

The appearance of Yahenni, Gonti and other Aetherborn is a conscious attempt to introduce agender characters into *Magic*. The Aetherborn present one problem, however: they are clearly alien. Even though they are humanoid and act human-like, many traits, like the fact that they are born of Aether and their lifespans are unnaturally short, still mark them as "other".

I perceive this as a trap many writers fall into. A writer who decides to introduce a character or a group of characters in order to represent a minority still separates this minority as "special". Even though a marginalised group is portrayed in the story, in the eyes of the audience it remains "other". It's the Aetherborn who are non-binary, but humans always fall into the binary categories.

A way out, in an ideal scenario, would be to have a non-binary character hail from among the "norm". We are facing exactly the same problem I mentioned above with female characters. The character in question should not be made special by being agender; they should be special because of their own powers and role in the story, while at the same time happening to be agender as well.

A positive application of such attitude was the case of the first transgender character to appear in a modern *Magic* story,[17] the Khan Alesha from Tarkir. Her clan, the Mardu, are raiders with a strong sense of community. In "*The Truth of Names*" (Wyatt 2015), we are told about the Mardu's custom of choosing their "war name" after they have proven themselves in battle. Alesha, perceived by others as a male

---

17. Technically, there was a significant "transgender" character already in the "old era" of *Magic* storytelling. In an early novel *Planeswalker* (Abbey 1998), there was a character named Xantcha, who follows the Planeswalker Urza. However, she starts as a Phyrexian construct, therefore having no gender to begin with, until later she decides to appropriate female gender. Strictly speaking, we cannot talk about "transgender" here, perhaps only in regards to the process of defining one's own identity. "Her physiology and resulting experience with sex and gender are all pretty radically different from real-world trans people." (Medwin 2015)

warrior,[18] chose the name of her grandmother. Her gender identity is mentioned casually, being seamlessly woven into the narrative; however, defining one's identity is a major theme in the story. Alesha, in fact, defines her identity twice: first, by choosing her female name (therefore, picking her gender identity) and later, at the end of the story, by getting her full "war name" with the epithet "Alesha, Who Smiles At Death". Medwin (2015) commended the story in particular for not being just a "trans story" and for creating a universally relatable protagonist who also happens to be transgender.

SEXUALITY IN MAGIC

Sexuality has never been an important topic in *Magic: The Gathering*. The game itself hasn't provided space for it, even though recently the developers started occasionally making cards representing couples instead of portraying them on separate cards.[19] In the story, it has appeared intermittently; in the story-driven era, the romantic involvement of

---

18. "She had been so different—only sixteen, a boy in everyone's eyes but her own, about to choose and declare her name before the khan and all the Mardu." (Wyatt 2015)

19. Namely "Anax and Cymede" (*Theros*), "Pia and Kiran Nalaar" (*Magic: Origins*) and "Kynaios and Tiro of Meletis" (*Commander 2016 Edition*). The *Commander (2016 Edition)* supplementary set has introduced a new card mechanic, "Partner", which allows players to play two commanders together for the Commander game format. This partnership does not imply sexual partnership, but it can be interpreted as such, and the card "Kynaios and Tiro of Meletis", printed in the same set and intended to work as an alternative for the Partner mechanic, features a couple.

characters has been hinted at rather than being an important factor in the plot.

Nevertheless, among recent trends, we can see the push for inclusion also with regards to sexuality. Characters belonging to sexual orientation minorities have appeared and have been presented as organic parts of the world(s), including nameless background characters.[20]

Sexual minorities are not ostracised, not even by the villains; their orientation is simply accepted as a natural part of who they are. The narrative does not draw any further attention to a character's sexual orientation other than what is part of the story. According to Beyer (2013), the first reference to a same-sex couple on a card appeared in "*Guardians of Meletis*" from *Theros*. The picture shows two statues of men and flavour text on the card reads: "The histories speak of two feuding rulers whose deaths were celebrated and whose monuments symbolised the end of their wars. In truth they were peaceful lovers, their story lost to the ages." The actual rulers appeared in the supplementary set *Commander (2016 Edition)* on the card "Kynaios and Tiro of Meletis". *Theros*'s flavour as a world inspired by Greek mythology made a gay couple fit the setting naturally, but Magic did not hesitate to introduce same-sex couples into other settings as well. The protagonists of *Shadows Over Innistrad*'s opening story, "*Under the Silver Moon*" (Kreines 2016b), are Halana and Alena, female werewolf hunters who share a romantic relationship. In *Kaladesh*, the

---

20. Such as a florist in the story "Catching Up" who, after trying to sell flowers to the protagonists, turns to an unknown gay couple: "'Sir!' said the woman, already working the couple behind them. 'Sir! A flower for your boyfriend there?'" (Kreines 2005a)

elderly artificer Mrs Pashiri is known to have had a wife.[21] These are all singular cases which, however, once again mark Wizards of the Coast's aim of inclusivity.

Conclusion

The *Magic* story shows several rare features among today's fantasy and sci-fi culture, including literature, films, television series and games. First of those is the obvious prominence of female characters, who appear as protagonists in over 50% of the *Magic* stories. The central cast of *Magic* – the Gatewatch, established with the new model of storytelling - features three female and two male Planeswalkers. Equal representation is shown even among minor characters in the story.

Magic does not hesitate to portray female characters in roles not traditionally considered to be natural for them, such as warriors, leaders or inventors. Unlike in many other fantasy and sci-fi stories, female authority in their respective fields is accepted and never challenged on the basis of their gender. Female characters in the story are active, not passive. *Magic* establishes an environment that is gender-non-discriminatory.

Equal treatment of characters of any gender can also be observed in the case of characters not belonging to the binary gender scheme. Nevertheless, the majority of the story still operates in terms of binary understanding of gender. At the same time, as shown in the case of Karn,

---

21. This is referred to in the story "Bottled Up" (Kreines 2006d). Her biography on the Kaladesh plane page reads: "(...) when she lost her wife, she took to working on her own designs in secret." (Wizards 2006)

the creators are actively trying to adjust the portrayal of characters where they believe they have erred because of a lack of awareness in the past. Communication with the larger player/reader community, who became more invested in the narrative after the story-driven shift, has certainly played an important role in this shift.

Treatment of characters of all genders and orientations as something natural creates a unique model to follow. I believe that, after stories that point out gender discrimination, the next stage is stories that treat characters of different gender, non-binary characters, or sexual minorities, equally. In any case, such an approach offers an alternative to the current status quo, because it portrays a kind of ideal world, in which no person is treated on the basis of their gender or sexuality, but according to other qualities relevant for their life and their story. That kind of approach creates "utopian literature" in the truest sense. No genre is better suited for portraying such a setting than fantasy, which is capable of transcending daily reality. On the contrary, it seems strange that much of fantasy and science fiction still submits to the stereotypes of our world in terms of gender and sexuality, while at the same time subverting more tangible and fundamental structures, such as laws of physics.

Magic is still not at that level yet, but it is getting there. And since "there" is not, in my opinion, a place, but rather a direction, it could serve as a positive inspiration and pointer towards greater inclusion in fantasy and in the gaming industry.

Bibliography

Abbey, L., 1998. *Planeswalker*. Wizards of the Coast.

Beyer, D., 2010. The Eldrazi Arisen. [online] Available at: <http://magic.wizards.com/en/articles/archive/feature/eldrazi-arisen-2010-03-29-0> [Accessed 15 December 2016].

Beyer, D., 2013. *Are the Guardians or [sic] Meletis Magic's first gay couple?* [online] Available at: <http://dougbeyermtg.tumblr.com/post/61385493599/are-the-guardians-or-meletis-magics-first-gay> [Accessed 15 December 2016].

Beyer, D., 2016. *Ebooks and the accessibility of Magic's story*. [online] Available at: <http://dougbeyermtg.tumblr.com/post/149686581984/ebooks-and-the-accessibility-of-magics-story> [Accessed 15 December 2016].

Fornazari, M. and Macedo, L., 2016. Gender Representation in Trading Card Games: Women and Men in Magic the Gathering. *Revista Estudos Anglo-Americanos*, [e-journal] vol. 45 no. 1:154-174. Available through: Academia website <https://www.academia.edu/25960256/GENDER_REPRESENTATION_IN_TRADING_CARD_GAMES_WOMEN_AND_MEN_IN_MAGIC_THE_GATHERING> [Accessed 8 December 2016].

Gastil, J., 1990. Generic Pronouns and Sexist Language: The Oxymoronic Character of Masculine Generics. *Sex Roles* 23 (11-12):629-643.

Kreines, K.J. ed., 2015a. *Prologue to Battle for Zendikar: Collected Stories*. [online] Available at: <http://magic.wizards.com/en/articles/archive/feature/magic-fiction-ebook-collection-2015-09-23> [Accessed 20 February 2017].

Kreines, K.J. ed., 2015b. *Origins: Collected Stories*. [online] Available at: <http://magic.wizards.com/en/articles/archive/feature/magic-fiction-ebook-collection-2015-09-23> [Accessed 20 February 2017].

Kreines, K.J. ed., 2015c. *Battle for Zendikar: Collected Stories*. [online] Available at: <http://magic.wizards.com/en/articles/archive/magic-story/battle-zendikar-story-summary-2015-12-23> [Accessed 20 February 2017].

Kreines, K.J. ed., 2016a. *Oath of the Gatewatch: Collected Stories*.

[online] Available at: <http://magic.wizards.com/en/articles/archive/feature/oath-gatewatch-story-summary-2016-03-02> [Accessed 20 February 2017].

Kreines, K.J. ed., 2016b. *Shadows Over Innistrad: Collected Stories*. [online] Available at: <http://magic.wizards.com/en/content/shadows-over-innistrad-story> [Accessed 20 February 2017].

Kreines, K.J. ed., 2016c. *Eldritch Moon: Collected Stories*. [online] Available at: <http://magic.wizards.com/en/content/eldritch-moon-story> [Accessed 20 February 2017].

Kreines, K.J. ed., 2016d. *Kaladesh: Collected Stories*. [online] Available at: <http://magic.wizards.com/en/content/kaladesh-story> [Accessed 20 February 2017].

Medwin, A., 2015. *Six Questions About A Girl*. [online] Available at: <http://trulyaliem.tumblr.com/post/115144596347/six-questions-about-a-girl> [Accessed 9 January 2017].

Rosewater, M., 2016a. *Hardly an hour ago you said Karn is genderless...*. [online] Available at: <http://markrosewater.tumblr.com/post/144437119558/hardly-an-hour-ago-you-said-karn-is-genderless> [Accessed 11 January 2017].

Rosewater, M., 2016b. *I'm personally loving all the new female planeswalkers...*. [online] Available at: <http://markrosewater.tumblr.com/post/146408959183/im-personally-loving-all-the-new-female> [Accessed 6 December 2016].

Wyatt, J., 2015. The Truth of Names. [online] Available at: <https://magic.wizards.com/en/articles/archive/magic-story/truth-names-2015-01-28> [Accessed 15 December 2016].

Wizards Of The Coast, 2016. *"Kaladesh", Magic: The Gathering*. [online] Available at: <http://magic.wizards.com/en/story/planes/kaladesh> [Accessed 15 December 2016].

Wizards Of The Coast, ongoing. *"Magic's Story", Magic: The Gathering*. [online] Available at: <http://magic.wizards.com/en/articles/columns/magic-story> [Accessed 20 February 2017].

Martin, G.R.R., 1996-2011. *A Song of Ice and Fire*. New York: Bantam Books.

What about Tauriel? From Divine Mothers to Active Heroines - The female roles in J. R. R. Tolkien's Legendarium and Peter Jackson's movie adaptations

By Jyrki Korpua

J. R. R. Tolkien's fiction is often considered to be male-dominated. Tolkien's Legendarium - his writings on Middle-earth - has its background in medieval myths and romances, where gender identities are quite conservative in the eyes of the Western 21st century reader. At a glance, Tolkien's stories seem to consider male characters as dominant and active, and female characters as passive. Representations of gender roles are therefore seemingly old fashioned. Perhaps because of this conservative attitude, the treatment of gender in Peter Jackson's film adaptations of both The Lord of the Rings and The Hobbit has been challenged. In the first movie, Jackson changed the male character of Glorfindel to the active female character of Arwen and, in The Hobbit he created a brand new female character, Tauriel. These changes have been scrutinised by both fans and scholars on numerous occasions.

This article focuses on the question of female roles in Tolkien's Legendarium and the corresponding Jackson movie adaptations. Firstly, I will examine female characters and their roles in Tolkien's main opus, before discussing the changes to the roles introduced by Peter Jackson's adaptations. Secondly, I will examine how audiences have reacted to the female roles in the movie series, concentrating on the non-canonical character of Tauriel. The latter part of my article is based on the results from the Finnish sub-project, to the global The World Hobbit Project, which was a study on audience reception. Although I am using

Finnish data as a background for my reading, these figures echo the results that can be seen in the global data.

Introduction: Female roles in Tolkien's Legendarium

John Ronald Reuel (J. R. R.) Tolkien (1892–1973) is the most influential fantasy writer of our time and perhaps the greatest mythographer of the 20th century. Tolkien's *Legendarium*[1] – most importantly his two main fantasy works, *The Lord of the Rings* (1954–55) and *The Hobbit, or There and Back Again* (1937) – changed the whole concept of fantasy in the 20th century. Fantasy became a major genre and since then, fantasy fiction has often ended up mimicking Tolkien's works.

Because of Tolkien's major role in the genre of fantasy, it was no surprise that Peter Jackson's movie series, *The Lord of the Rings* (2001–2003) and *The Hobbit* (2012–14), became extremely popular.[2] However, despite their success

---

1. Originally, a *legendarium* was a book or series of books comprising a collection of legends. Tolkien himself used the word *legendarium* to refer to his writing concerning his fictional fantasy world of Middle-earth, in a letter to Milton Waldman in 1951 (Tolkien, 1999:xvii). Since then, the word *legendarium* has become commonly used by Tolkien scholars in place of "Tolkien mythology". I use the word *Legendarium* to describe all Tolkien's texts that deal with Middle-earth, although I am aware that sometimes in Tolkien studies *legendarium* is used to specifically denote Tolkien's Elvish legends, and that *The Lord of the Rings* and *The Hobbit* are not considered a part of these. For me, all Tolkien's texts concerning the legends of Elves (e.g. *The Silmarillion*) and the fictional history of Hobbits (*The Hobbit* and *The Lord of the Rings*) form a complete and coherent *legendarium*.

2. Despite there being only three movies, *The Lord of the Rings* series is one of the most successful movie franchises in history. According

and their high audience ratings in the *International Movie Database* (IMDB) (see Korpua, 2016:383), many fans of the books criticised the movies.

Tolkien's fiction and Jackson's adaptations are two very different forms of art. Tolkien's *Legendarium* was created (mostly) in the first part of the 20th century and reflected a much older, almost medieval imagery (see Sly, 2000:109; Shippey, 2003:5; Korpua, 2015:29). Jackson's movies were made, so it seems, for the action driven audiences of the 21th century. In the films, Tolkien's fiction was seen through a 'Hollywood lens', which usually concentrates on box office results. In contemporary Hollywood, the horizon of expectation usually ends up combining plenty of action with small portions of romance and humour. This is also clear when comparing the number of action scenes in Tolkien's books and in the movie adaptations. The books concentrate more on describing the milieus, creating a plausible background for the story and then slowly revealing the plot, while building tension for the forthcoming climax. In the movie versions, fighting scenes, constant chases and other stunts are, from early on, central devices for the plot. Then some elements of romance and affection are added to this 'soup' of action sequences. Of course, this results in stories that differ in ways to what Tolkien originally wrote.

---

to McCarthy (2015), in North America it is almost as successful as monolithic movie franchises such as *James Bond* and *Star Wars*. *The Hobbit* series is also very successful, with nearly three billion dollars of global box office revenues (see Box Office Mojo). When combined, *The Lord of the Rings* and *The Hobbit* are the third most successful movie franchise after the *Marvel Cinematic Universe* and the *Harry Potter* series.

The pressing question for our purposes is, what happened to female roles in the process of 'adaptation'?[3]

At first glance, Tolkien's stories seem to present male characters as dominant and active and female characters as passive. Perhaps because of this conservative attitude, the treatment of 'male' and 'female' roles[4] was challenged in Peter Jackson's adaptations of both *The Lord of the Rings* and *The Hobbit*. In the first series, Jackson transformed the male character of Glorfindel into the active female character of Arwen and, in *The Hobbit* he created a new female character, Tauriel. These changes have been scrutinised by both fans and scholars.

Despite the conservative, male-dominated imagery, there are also active females in Tolkien's fiction. These are, in a way, described in a reimagined medieval tone, as archetypes of certain mythic motifs.[5] The most obvious examples are the characters of Galadriel and Éowyn in *The Lord of the Rings*. Galadriel, a powerful Elven lady and the ruler of her domain, is an archetypal representation of the Virgin Mary; she is a mythical 'Divine Mother' in the *Legendarium*. In

---

3. Adaptation here is used in the broad understanding of the concept. Although *The Lord of the Rings* movie series is somewhat faithful to original work that it is based on, *The Hobbit* series is, in my opinion, more of a large budget fan fiction movie using *The Hobbit* and other parts of Tolkien's *Legendarium* as its main source.

4. It's important to keep in mind that there are other gender roles to these two, and that characters in Tolkien's fiction are in many occasions "non-human" (Hobbits, Elves, Dwarves, Orcs, etc.) and should not be judged by these stereotypical gender limitations.

5. An archetype is considered to be the original pattern or model on which all things of the same kind are based. Northrop Frye sees some mythic figures (or metaphors) as this kind of communicable symbol (Frye, 1967:118).

his letter to Ruth Austin in the year 1971, Tolkien admitted that he used the Virgin Mary as background for Galadriel, the most powerful Elf in *The Lord of the Rings* and in the Third Age of Middle-earth. Of course, the similarities between Mary and Galadriel are only superficial and, on an idealogical level, not on a par in the narrative:

> *I think it is true that I owe much of this character [Galadriel] to Christian and Catholic teaching and imagination about Mary, but actually Galadriel was a penitent: in her youth a leader in the rebellion against the Valar (the angelic guardians). At the end of the First Age she proudly refused forgiveness or permission to return. She was pardoned because of her resistance to the final and overwhelming temptation to take the Ring for herself.* (Carpenter, 1981:407. See also Korpua, 2015:160-161)

There are other examples of this "Divine Mother" archetype, such as Varda, the Queen of Stars, and Melian, the lady of Doriath in Tolkien's *The Silmarillion*. In *The Silmarillion*, there are also other active female characters. I consider these characters "active" because their actions transform the plot and the narrative. For example, Lúthien, the heroine in the story "Beren and Lúthien", or Haleth the Hunter, Chieftain of the Haladin. The number of active female characters may be small, but nonetheless important. Of these, Lúthien is the most significant. In *The Silmarillion*, Beren and Lúthien steal one of the Silmarils back from Melkor. Beren is the greatest human hero in *The Silmarillion*, and Lúthien is a "semi-angelic" being, because her father is the Elven king Thingol, and her mother, Melian, is one the Maiar, the spirits who govern Middle-earth. In the story, Beren and Lúthien manage to steal one of the Silmarils from Melkor's crown, thanks to Lúthien's singing, which puts Melkor and all of his court to sleep. (Tolkien, 1999:212-213)

If we interpret Galadriel as the most central example of the "divine mother" archetype, Éowyn in *The Lord of the Rings* represents the other type of feminine archetype: a fighting, Valkyrie-like female heroine. This kind of medieval mythic archetype resembles the active heroines of folk stories, such as the Viking Queen Olga or Hua Mulan from Chinese ballads. Still, it took a long time for these active heroines of folk stories to seep into mainstream media products. In *The Lord of the Rings*, Éowyn's participation in the War of the Rings is also a premonition of many later active female warriors of the fantasy genre, such as Xena the Warrior Princess and Buffy the Vampire Slayer from their respective popular TV-series, or Elektra, from Marvel comics (see also Innes, 1999). In the movies, it has been said that this kind of strong female warrior only emerged after characters such as Ellen Ripley (act. Sigourney Weaver) in *Alien* (dir. Ridley Scott, 1979) and Sarah Connor (act. Linda Hamilton) in *Terminator* (dir. James Cameron, 1984). (Helford, 2000:65)

Still, despite, for example, Suzanne Collins' Kattnis Everdeen (act. Jennifer Lawrence) from the extremely successful *Hunger Games* novels, and subsequent movies, strong female characters seem to be in decline at the moment. (see Conrad, 2011:79-81; Lauzen, 2014:1-2)

In Tolkien's *Legendarium*, female characters are rare. Because of that, necessary changes in roles have been applied to the movie adaptations. It can be said that, whereas Éowyn is not the only active female heroine in Tolkien's fiction, she is still a rare exception. For this reason, Peter Jackson tried to emphasise the roles of some female characters, e.g. Arwen, and introduced a non-canonical one, Tauriel, in the movie versions.

Changes in the roles

In the movie version of *The Lord of the Rings*, the main female characters are Arwen, Galadriel and Éowyn. Galadriel and Éowyn are in many ways similar to the characters appearing in the books, but Arwen is a changed and re-imagined character. Éowyn and Galadriel are portrayed quite faithfully to Tolkien's texts. In *Tolkien on Film: Essays on Peter Jackson's The Lord of the Rings* (2005), Cathy Akers-Jordan, Jane Chance, Victoria Gaydosik, and Maureen Thum all contended that the portrayal of Arwen and other women in the Jackson films is overall thematically faithful to (or compatible with) Tolkien's writings, despite the differences.

I beg to differ. The changes in Arwen's character are drastic. In *The Lord of the Rings*, Tolkien describes Arwen as queenly, divine and remote:

...there was a chair under a canopy, and there sat a lady fair to look upon, and so like was she in form of womanhood to Elrond that Frodo guessed she was one of his close kindred. Young was she and yet not so. The braids of her dark hair were touched by no frost; her white arms and clear face were flawless and smooth, and the light of stars was in her bright eyes,

> *grey as a cloudless night; yet queenly she looked, and thought and knowledge were in her glance, as of one who has known many things that the years bring. - - Such loveliness in living thing Frodo had never seen before nor imagined in his mind...* (Tolkien, 1995:221)

In the movie version, Arwen is changed to be a warrior-like princess who gives away her immortality to be with Aragorn, the future king. For an immortal Elf, this is a huge sacrifice. This loss of immortality can be read (in some ways) also from Tolkien's texts, although it is not that simple to interpret. There, the change concerning mortality/immortality is quite central. Tolkien wrote in some occasions that for their love in this world, Aragorn and Arwen had to pay the ultimate cost. In Appendix A of *The Lord of the Rings*, Aragorn dies. The last words that he says to Arwen are, "In sorrow we must go, but not in despair. Behold! We are not bound forever to the circles of the world, and beyond them is more than memory! Farewell!" (Tolkien, 1995:1038). Arwen dies too, since Tolkien writes (ibid.) that "she laid herself to rest upon Cerin Amroth; and there is her green grave, until the world is changed, and all the days of her life are utterly forgotten by men that come after". Then again, there are also Elves in Tolkien's *Legendarium* who decide to die and leave this earth. So we do not know from these sources whether Arwen (like her grand-uncle Elros, the first King of Numénor) decided to die the death of Men or died willingly as an Elf.

Still, the change in the character of Arwen from a divine and remote "princess" to an active warrior who fights the

Nazgûl in the wilderness and defeats them at the Ford of Bruinen did not matter to the big audience. In the books, Arwen was only a supporting character in a small, though important role. Also, the removal of the character of Glorfindel had already been done in Ralph Bakshi's animated version of *The Lord of the Rings* (1978). There, Glorfindel's character was melted into the character of Legolas. In that adaptation, it was Legolas who protected Frodo against the Nazgûl at the Ford of Bruinen, not Glorfindel. So, changing the character of Glorfindel to someone else was not a new thing in adaptations, and it was a clever way to both introduce the character of Arwen, the future Queen, and also to introduce a rare active female character to the series.

Remote mothers

After a closer look at both Tolkien's texts and Jackson's movies, it becomes clear that the most important female characters are "remote mothers". They are gone - dead or disappeared. Like so many central characters in myths or fantasy, both Bilbo Baggins in *The Hobbit* and Frodo Baggins in *The Lord of the Rings* are orphans, as of course was J. R. R. Tolkien himself. Both Bilbo and Frodo are bachelors who do not have that much contact with females. In fact, Frodo is the adopted heir of Bilbo, because Frodo's parents, Drogo and Primula, had been killed in a boating accident. Frodo's mother, Primula, is not referenced much, but Bilbo's mother, Belladonna Took, is often mentioned, even though she doesn't appear in the text as an active character. She is referred to as "one of the three remarkable daughters of Old Took", and Humphrey Carpenter (1977:175) even draws an analogy between Belladonna and Tolkien's own mother, Mabel. This is an interesting analogy, since in the film series of *The Hobbit*, Belladonna Took is mentioned many times as an influential character in Bilbo's life, and pictures of her can be seen in two different adaptations: in *The Lord of the Rings: The Fellowship of the Ring* (2001) and in *The Hobbit: The Battle of the Five Armies* (2014). In both movies, the picture of Belladonna is based on the look of Fran Walsh, the wife of Jackson and the co-writer of both movie series. Still, in the movies, once again, the mothers are usually gone or absent. In *The Hobbit* movies, the screenplay pays attention to many "absent mothers": we find the mother of Bilbo, a reference to the mother of Kili (one of the dwarves), and also a short but interesting discussion on the (non-canonical) mother of Legolas, the absent wife of King Thranduil. Also, we might start to wonder where the wife of Bard is, who is the mother of his children? Even the ancestral mother of the monstrous giant spider Ungoliant is mentioned in the movies. In Tolkien's fiction there are several "absent mothers" types. Also, there is an important reference to the grandmother of Gollum, a matriarch of his family, who drives Gollum out of his community because of his actions.

Mothers and grandmothers have been active, but not in the texts themselves. Only their past actions are mentioned, but now they are almost (physically) invisible. An interesting question is why they are gone? One possible answer is that movies of this length have no room for (stereotypically portrayed) tender and caring mothers. The main characters are better off as unattached orphans. Maybe their actions are then more easily understood by the audience. The loss of motherly care can be seen as one aspect of tragedy for some characters; for example, Legolas, Bilbo, and even Gollum, who is driven into the wilderness by his grandmother. Even affection for late mothers is criticised in the movies. As Gandalf says to Bilbo in *The Hobbit: An Unexpected Journey*: "When did doilies and your mother's dishes become so important to you?"

So, is there room for active heroines?

Non-canonical Tauriel

As said earlier, the changes in the representation of Arwen in *The Lord of the Rings* weren't scrutinised that closely by the audience. However, after *The Hobbit* filmisations, there were many quite aggressive comments by the audience focused on the character of Tauriel. In the movies, Tauriel is a Wood Elf of Mirkwood and Captain of the Elven Guard of King Thranduil's Woodland Realm.

Tauriel does not appear in any of Tolkien's texts, therefore she is considered to be a so-called "non-canonical" character, added perhaps by Peter Jackson and his team to introduce a female perspective and give female viewers a chance to identify with her. Her being non-canonical has become one major part of the discussion.

Of course, there are a couple of crucial reasons for Jackson's team to insert this character:

1. *The Hobbit* was first read aloud to Tolkien's own children. Later, it was published as a fantastic adventure novel for young readers. At first, the publisher thought that it was aimed at small boys

aged 5-7.
2. There are virtually no female characters in the book. As a matter of fact, there are also very few actual human characters in the book.

Tauriel's character has been criticised in survey answers for the following reasons:
1. Unneeded addition. Does not bring anything important to the movies. The addition of Legolas in *The Hobbit* films has been criticised on the same grounds.
2. 2) An action-heavy Tauriel (as well as all the other Elves) is non-realistic and the fight scenes are largely there because of game-lovers, children and teens who like these kinds of stunts.
3. 3) Tauriel and Kili's "love-affair" conflicts two important Elf-Dwarf relationships in *The Lord the Rings book*. Firstly, that Gimli and Legolas are the first Elves and Dwarves for thousands of years to form a friendship; secondly, that this love affair between Tauriel and Kili detracts from the unique beauty of Gimli's infatuation with Galadriel in *The Lord of the Rings*. This valid point was raised in many answers.

When analysing the data in our study, Tauriel is by far the most criticised and denounced character. Her small love affair with the Dwarf Kili is almost brutally dealt with in many of the survey answers.

Interpreting the audience responses in the Finnish data of the World Hobbit Project

Out of the total 1614 respondents of the Finnish survey, 293 mention Tauriel in their answers.[6] Altogether, Tauriel is mentioned 445 times in 353 different questions, which means that many of the participants have something to say about her in multiple answers. She is a highly discussed character, with an 18.26% survey presence. Moreover, 14 participants tell us that they have debated the character with their friends or on the Internet, or that they have followed the debates surrounding the character. In the tables below, we can observe the results concerning Tauriel, divided by different questions. I must add here that participants are allowed to mention Tauriel in an answer where they express their enjoyment of the movies, but still be negative towards the character.[7]

---

6. In the survey, there were 21 different questions in total. For more information on the survey and the project, see Barker & Mathijs, 2016. About the Finnish sub-project, it should be noted that the Finnish audience answered the survey in multiple languages. The majority of the answers were given in Finnish (1438), Swedish (37), and English (136) but there were also two participants who used Spanish (1) and Russian (1). In this article, I have translated all non-English answers where necessary. There was also one participant who answered the questionnaire in Danish, but only with check-box-answers, and no added text. As for other quantitative statistics on the Finnish data, at this stage I should note that, of all Finnish participants, 1078 answered 'Female' and 536 'Male' to the question, "Are you Male/Female?". On the statistics of the Finnish survey participants, see also Koistinen, Ruotsalainen & Välisalo, 2016.
7. The logic of open-ended answers is sometimes quite misleading. People can give negatively toned answers to positive questions or positively toned answers to negative questions. For example, participants can also

Table 1: Questions where Tauriel is mentioned: (353 different questions)

Disappointed by the movies	176
Favourite character in the movies	48
Impressed with the movies	46
Reasons for rating the movies	36
Broader themes in the movies	23
Reasons for debates created by the movies	14
Discussion on genre/genres of the movie	5
Imagined communities of the participant	3
Personal information of the participant	2

The reception of this added, non-canonical female character, is twofold and quite conflicting. In my own categorisations of these answers, 68 participants mention liking the character, 32 use neutral tones when mentioning Tauriel, and 193 participants mention disliking the character. This shows that the attitude towards Tauriel in this survey is divided among participants, whom I call "likers", "neutrals" and "dislikers".

---

mention in a question about favourite characters those whom they did not like. Or, in a question regarding "disappointment with the movie", they can also discuss those things that she or he liked about the movie. There are lots of these kinds of contradictory answers. For example, participant #4073, in the midst of answering a question concerning her or his favourite characters, includes why she or he hated another character: "Tauriel is just a female catalyst, who is added to the plot to enable the mandatory over-highlighted love triangle".

Table 2: "Likers", "Neutrals" and "Dislikers": (293 different participants)

Participants who like the character of Tauriel	68
Of these: Emphasise liking the romantic aspect	15
Of these: Emphasise liking the addition of a female character	20
Of these: Mentions Tauriel as her/his favourite character	33
Participants who were neutral on the character of Tauriel	32
Participants who did not like the character of Tauriel	193
Of these: Emphasise disliking the non-canonical (added) character	50
Of these: Emphasise disliking the romantic aspect	82
Of these: Emphasise disliking the "love triangle" of Tauriel, Kili, and Legolas	40
Of these: Emphasise dislike for the portrayal of Tauriel as an "object of love"	21

Conclusion: What about Tauriel?

So what about Tauriel? Her addition to the movie series was a brave but heavily scrutinised move. The survey's answers verify those observations; something that can also be seen from Internet discussions and articles (see for example Miyamoto 2013). In the survey's answers, under all categories, participants (42 to be specific) comment that Tauriel is "unneeded" or "unnecessary", so the attitude towards non-canonical characters is quite easily interpreted there. Still, of these, some participants remain neutral towards Tauriel or are contradictory. For example, participant #805 writes that Tauriel "was cute, although unnecessary"; or, "Romance was added there to attract certain audiences" (participant #1011).

Two people raise the importance of Tauriel's character and her romance with Kili as a possible allegorisation of minorities and/or queer themes. Also, six participants mention romance and love between Tauriel and Kili as a broader theme of the movies, which is of course non-canonical if compared to the book on which *The Hobbit* movies are based. Participant #1201 writes from a diverse and interesting angle on the subject of gender roles and queer readings:

> *I also like the theme about friendship and love across barriers like race, and especially that the films (including LOTR) make the subtext in queer couples so strong that it is almost text. I also like the fact that Thranduil is seen to perceive the affection between an Elf and a Dwarf as real because, no matter which reading of their relationship you prefer, it will make it easier for Legolas if he ever brings Gimli home to meet his father. So, for that reason, I like the fact that Tauriel was included and is a redhead. I also like the fact that they made an effort to show strong women who don't always have to be strong, in spite of the serious lack of female characters in the series. I loved the not-model-looking-woman (there needs to be more of those in films) who rallied up the women to join the fight.*

Along with this, her character is seen as a remote echo of Arwen from *The Lord of the Rings* movies. For example, participant #1842 comments that "Tauriel was just a copy of Arwen, and was not convincing as such."

Many complain about the fact that Tauriel was introduced in the movies to be an object of male desire (both Kili's and Legolas'). For example, participant #1096 is one of the 21 people who brings the question of gender roles to the fore. She writes that the character of Tauriel is questionable from a feminist point of view since, although she is a strong and tough character, she is still only created in the movies to be the object of Kili's and Legolas's romantic love. Many viewers observe this point.

There was certainly division of opinion on the character. For example (#1851) liked the fact that the Captain of the Guard was a woman because there were hardly any female characters in the movies. Then again, he/she doesn't like the romantic elements in the movies, and especially hates the love triangle between Legolas, Kili and Tauriel.

It can be summarised, therefore, that the main reason for disliking the character of Tauriel is usually the romantic plot, although some participants (15 in total) also mention liking it.

From the analysis of the survey's answers, it is possible to draw conclusions on the issue of female identity and roles in Tolkien's *Legendarium*, and the movie adaptations of his central works. 1) female identity in Tolkien's *Legendarium* is not that simplistic and stereotypical as it is sometimes portrayed to be but, despite that, 2) in Jackson's movies, even when possibly trying to change the status quo, the representations of female identity are quite simple-minded and females are often portrayed as either "absent mothers" or "active heroines". The latter is an attempt at creating gender harmony in action movies, but the characters still end up being objects of love or affection for male characters; as seems to be the case concerning Tauriel.

Bibliography

Box Office Mojo. *All Time Box Office*. [online] Available at: <http://www.boxofficemojo.com/alltime/world/> [Accessed 3 January 2017].

Barker, M. et al., 2014–15. *The World Hobbit Project*. [online survey] Aberystwyth.

Barker, M. and Mathjis, E., 2012. Researching world audiences: The experience of a complex methodology. *Participations - Journal of Audience & Reception Studies*, Volume 9, Issue 2:664–689.

Barker, M. & Mathjis, E., 2016. Introduction: The World Hobbit Project. *Participations - Journal of Audience & Reception Studies*, Volume 13, Issue 2:158–174.

Carpenter, H., 1977. *J. R. R. Tolkien. A Biography*. Boston: Houghton Mifflin Company.

Conrad, D., 2011. Femmes Futures. One Hundred Years of Female Representation in Sf Cinema. *Science Fiction Film and Television* Vol. 4, No.1:79–99.

Croft, J.B., ed., 2005. *Tolkien on Film: Essays on Peter Jackson's The Lord of the Rings*. Altadena: Mythopoeic Press.

Frye, N., 1967 (1957). *Anatomy of Criticism. Four Essays by Northrop Frye*. New York: Atheneum.

Helford, E.R., 2000. Introduction. In: E.R. Helford, ed. 2000. *Fantasy Girls. Gender in the New Universe of Science Fiction and Fantasy Television*. Lanham, MD: Rowman & Littlefield. 1–9.

Inness, S.A., 1999. *Tough Girls: Women Warriors and Wonder Women in Popular Culture*. Philadelphia: University of Pennsylvania Press.

Aino-Kaisa, K., Ruotsalainen, M. and Välisalo, T., 2016. The World Hobbit Project in Finland: Audience responses and transmedial user practices. *Participations - Journal of Audience & Reception Studies*, Volume 13, Issue 2:356–379.

Korpua, J., 2015. *Constructive Mythopoetics in J. R. R. Tolkien's Legendarium*. PhD. Oulu: University of Oulu Press. Available at: <http://jultika.oulu.fi/Record/isbn978-952-62-0928-9.> [Accessed 3 January

2017].

Korpua, J., 2016. Finnish audience responses to myth and mythology in The Hobbit: Connections between J R R Tolkien's fiction and Peter Jackson's The Hobbit film series. *Participations - Journal of Audience & Reception Studies*, Volume 13, Issue 2:380–392.

Lauzen, M.M., 2015. *It's a Man's (Celluloid) World: On-Screen Representations of Female Characters in the Top 100 Films of 2014*. [online] Center for the Study of Women in Television & Film. Available at: <http://womenintvfilm.sdsu.edu/files/2014_Its_a_Mans_World_Report.pdf> [Accessed 3 January 2017].

Mathews, R., 2002. *Fantasy. The Liberation of Imagination*. New York: Routledge.

McCarthy, N., 2015. *The Most Successful Movie Franchises In History [Infographic]*. [online] Available at: <http://www.forbes.com/sites/niallmccarthy/2015/04/13/the-most-successful-movie-franchises-in-history-infographic/#372f0b5f2ffc> [Accessed 3 January 2017].

Miyamoto, K., 2013. *The Tauriel/Kili romance seemed like a weak point in the movie. Do others agree with that? What was the point of including it?* [online] Available at: <https://www.quora.com/The-Tauriel-Kili-romance-seemed-like-a-weak-point-in-the-movie-Do-others-agree-with-that-What-was-the-point-of-including-it> [Accessed 3 January 2017].

Shippey, T., 2003. *The Road to Middle-earth. How J. R. R. Tolkien created a New Mythology*. Revised and expanded ed. New York: Houghton Mifflin Company.

Sly, D., 2000. Weaving Nets of Gloom: 'Darkness Profound' in Tolkien and Milton. In: G. Clark and D. Timmons, eds., 2000. *J. R. R. Tolkien and His Literary Resonances. Views of Middle-earth*. Westport: Greenwood Press. 109–120.

Tolkien, J. R. R., 1975 (1951). *The Hobbit, or There and Back Again*. New Edition. London: George Allen & Unwin Ltd.

Carpenter, H., ed., 1981. *The Letters of J. R. R. Tolkien*, with the assistance of Christopher Tolkien. London: George Allen & Unwin Ltd.

Tolkien, J. R. R. 1995 (1954–55). *The Lord of the Rings*. 4th ed. London: HarperCollinsPublishers.

Tolkien, J. R. R., 1999 (1977). *The Silmarillion*. C. Tolkien ed. London: HarperCollinsPublishers.

Newly Added Female Characters to Blockbuster Franchises: Gender Balancing in Otherwise Male-Dominated Fictional Worlds or a Greater Purpose?

By Alina Hadîmbu

With gender equality being one of the most sensitive topics of the 21st century, the world of fantasy and fiction on the silver screen has seen a surge in the number of female characters in leading roles. The main question is: are these characters added solely for the purpose of having a balanced male/female count and screen time, or is there more? Do these newly added female characters bring a solid contribution, change destinies, change the world perhaps, or are they only inscribed for more traditional roles (for example, serving as love interests)? Two very recent examples serve to show that such female characters are far from lacking in substance. We will have an in-depth look at the creation and mission of Rey, the new leading character in the latest Star Wars trilogy, and Tauriel, a non-canonical heroine added to The Hobbit film adaptations based on J.R.R. Tolkien's books. This paper will explore their personalities, purpose and interactions with other characters, as well as their impact on the unfolding events, as presented in their respective high-grossing films.

Introduction

Some of the highest grossing film productions of recent years inscribed to long-living fandoms (Middle-earth and Star Wars) have advanced new and compelling female characters, despite the pressures of keeping their fictional universes unaltered.

The change appears to have been dictated by a need to have strong, representative females to balance these fictional worlds and meet the demands of contemporary works of fiction. The audience either views this as necessary, given the efforts to create equality between genders, or voices their opinions against it, seeing the change as an unneeded alteration of the original fictional universe. The "purists" are thus in conflict with gender-concerned fans. However, the aim of this analysis is not to find out which of the two groups is right, but to figure out whether there is substance to these recently invented characters or not.

This study aims to focus on two recent blockbuster films representing decades-old fictional universes: *The Hobbit* and *Star Wars*. We are going to explore the idea that well written female characters with a genuine purpose can successfully represent an otherwise male dominated fictional world, without compromising the fan experience in a universe which has been familiar to the public for decades.

The Hobbit (Tolkien, 1037) book was considered as not fully suitable for a 21st century screen blockbuster, unless it was enriched with female characters. The book, inspired by J.R.R. Tolkien's own war experiences, features thirteen male Dwarves, a male Hobbit, a male wizard and male Elves. Screenplay writers make use of additional Tolkien material to introduce female Elf Galadriel in connected, but rather brief, scenes. The team also decided to add a completely new, non-canonical character – Tauriel, an Elven warrior female who appears to be the love interest of two male heroes. While plenty argue that it does not serve the narrative to introduce a female character just to please the audience, we can easily observe that Tauriel serves a much greater purpose.

A look at the other trilogy, *Star Wars* (2015-ongoing) shows us yet another new female character in the limelight: Rey, whose purpose, method of action and mindset make her a well written and well received creation – without seeming to be there just to fulfil an agenda.

Do Females Only Serve as Romantic Interest / Mere Feminine Presence?

Rey, Female Lead in the New Star Wars Trilogy

Rey is a scavenger left behind by her family on planet Jakku. Right from the beginning, she is stoic, has a kind heart and a great will to do the right thing in every situation. She has a good moral compass. As the story progresses, Rey, whose history has not been revealed yet, proves to be Force sensitive and very promising in this regard. It is thus a departure from Princess Leia, who, although was in a family of Force users, never employed such powers herself.

J.J. Abrams and writer Lawrence Kasdan discussed the concept of a female lead for the new trilogy in the following terms: "We always wanted to write Rey as the central character" (Pulver, 2015). Therefore it was decided from the very beginning that the movie was to have a woman in the main slot. Dušan Lazarević, when talking about his impressions of the character, added: "She showed a combination of vulnerability and strength which gave her a complexity" (Saner, 2015). In addition, another director, Colin Trevorrow, mentioned that Rey's origin and story are "deeply and profoundly satisfying" and that Rey is "important in this universe (...), in the entire galaxy. She deserves this" (Chitwood, 2016). Rey is not a sidekick, but a complete, highly important character, standing on her own. Composer John Williams explained that he did not wish to create a love theme for Rey, but a mature and adventurous one. Furthermore, the heroine is described as a "loner, hothead, gear-head, badass" by screenwriter Michael Arndt (Tracey, 2015).

Rey does not have any romantic involvement so far. It is Finn who tries to flirt with her, but she remains focused on the job at hand through and through. In the end, the viewers get to see their honest friendship and loyalty. There is no hint of Rey being interested romantically in anyone at all.

Tauriel's Greater Role in The Hobbit Trilogy

With Tauriel, the situation is much different. It is clearly stated that Legolas had started to favour her, while the Dwarf Kili was entirely swept off his feet at the sight of the beautiful Elf. At the moment of his death, Tauriel kissing his lips could be a clear indicator of the romantic feelings being reciprocated, yet we can argue it was too soon for such feelings to have developed. The problem with this female character is that it seems to bring the romance to the fore. It is the reason why purists rejected this addition and saw it as below Tolkien's standards. A good look at the film, however, reveals a much deeper purpose for Tauriel.

Until the reshoot, there was no intention at all to have Tauriel in a romantic triangle. Evangeline Lilly's agreement to take on the role was in fact based on this, as confessed in an interview (Lash, 2013). This clearly shows that her character was not introduced because the movie lacked romance, but because of other needs. Besides that, Tauriel goes against the grain – she is very different from all Elves seen in the movies, which tend to act the same way, have similar ideals and are obedient to their rulers. She is a nonconformist who often acts on impulse and rebels against the known social order. (Rottenberg, 2013)

Beyond the Mary Sue: The Victory of Unique Feminine Powers

It is safe to say that Legolas being in love with Tauriel is only a pretext for her bigger role in the story. The romance is rather a sub-plot; the story can do without it, but what this Elven guard does apart from that makes her a catalyst. The Elf maiden is the only character who dares to stand up to Thranduil and speak against his selfish, ignorant politics. The Elf king fails to see the threat extending over Middle-earth and has no concern for anything outside his kingdom. Worse, he is cold and detached even to those closest to him, including his own son, Legolas. Thranduil mistreats Thorin in an unforgivable way, mocking his royalty, stopping his noble mission, placing no value on his life and, in the end, threatening him with war in order to obtain his part of the treasure. Thranduil's arrogance and cheating ways finally meet a strong opposing voice in Tauriel. Risking her own life, the Elf maiden tries to awaken the king to the realities of the world and the wrongs of his ways. She takes orders with a keen sense of responsibility, but stops doing so when these orders do not fall in line with her sense of fairness.

Her stern commitment to standing for the truth inspires Legolas to do the same and follow her into exile. Tauriel constantly puts her life in danger in order to do the right thing, to fight the enemy and save the good ones – even when she is forbidden to do so.

However, Tauriel is not necessarily renowned for her fighting skills or courage, or for speaking the truth. It is about the way she handles the completely feminine traits, which are often seen as weaknesses. No matter how strong and cunning in battle, she lets her femininity shine through, as gracefully as Rey did. She is not ashamed to be compassionate. In fact, she goes much deeper and analyses Thranduil enough to find out he is deeply flawed. "There is no love in you", says Tauriel in the movie – a statement that infuriates the king. The viewer knows that she is right. Actor Lee Pace succeeds in portraying the king as heartless, cold and detached. He does not even care about the feelings and the happiness of his own son, who is forbidden to have romantic involvement with someone socially below him. Tauriel is thus the voice of conscience, the voice of truth. She allows herself to empathise with the prisoners and hear their stories. Tauriel knows when to listen and when to speak (always from the heart); she knows when to fight and when to drop weapons. She is not afraid to cry and to ask why love hurts so much; in allowing her feminine power to shine through, she becomes an agent of change. Thranduil himself is softened; he comes in contact with his own long forgotten feelings of love and pain. He is inspired to acknowledge that love is a very real force.

Rey's Role in Balancing the Force

Since the audience has only seen the first instalment of the trilogy at this point, there is a lot of mystery surrounding newcomer Rey. Fan theories suggest that she may be either a Skywalker or a Palpatine, especially due to her Force sensitivity. However, Rey's raw emotions make her a suitable candidate for the Dark Side and so both Kylo Ren and Supreme Master Snoke are interested in capturing her alive and convincing her to join them. We may conclude then that Rey is more than just a female added to the story to balance the gender distribution.

Rey's connection to Finn appears as a one-sided budding romance – since only Finn expresses interest. We see her as friendly, yet disinterested, and entirely focused on her mission. At the same time, she is capable of showing devotion and great respect and care for her male allies. Rey is also a hyper-competent girl, which may paint her as a "Mary Sue", but that can, and surely will, be explained in Episode VIII or IX through revealing her parents and the source of her abilities.

Rey's innocence is endearing. There is no mean arrogance in her. She is often childish and sweet, sometimes afraid and hopeless. It is a very human, realistic portrayal in this regard. She is sometimes exceedingly happy about accomplishments, such as fixing and flying ships, but gets a reality check from Han Solo, which is fun to watch. Thus, Rey is not a know-it-all, nor a self-absorbed person. She is rather a simple, innocent and honest girl trying to perform good actions in every situation. That said, she does have remarkable Force abilities.

Conclusion

The addition of new female characters to the blockbusters *Star Wars* and *The Hobbit* may have been done with the purpose of balancing the male/female ratio in these movies. It may also have happened as an answer to the demand for strong female leads. However, besides all that, we are dealing with well-written characters with a profound, complex purpose. The femininity is present and honoured in them both. With Rey, *Star Wars* fans finally have the Force sensitivity manifesting in a female character with a mission. The tension created, and the many questions surrounding her origin and consequent evolution, are at the core of the fandom at the moment – something that shows how skilfully her character has been built. Tauriel is the Elf who brings balance in Mirkwood when its king closes his heart to all compassion and who strives to create the unity that is needed more than ever. They both stand alone and any romantic involvement (or friendship) does not detract from that. In fact, both characters exist and make sense in their fictional worlds even with such story arcs completely ignored.

Bibliography

Chitwood, A., 2016. *Star Wars Episode IX Director Colin Trevorrow Promises Satisfying Answers to Rey Theories.* [online] Available at: <http://collider.com/star-wars-9-rey-parents-colin-trevorrow/Final AH.doc> [Accessed 12 January 2017].

Foster, A.D., 2016. *Star Wars: The Force Awakens.* New York: Del Rey.

Hanslip, A. and Svilpis, A., 1993. *An Uncharted Land: Female Characters in J. R. R. Tolkien's 'The Lord of the Rings' and Related Writings.* Calgary: ProQuest Dissertations Publishing.

Helen, D., 2014. *Tauriel Actress describes Love Triangle as Not Totally Tolkien.* [online] Available at: <https://www.tolkiensociety.org/2014/07/tauriel-actress-describes-love-triangle-as-not-totally-tolkien> [Accessed 24 November 2016].

Lash, J., 2013. *Evangeline Lilly on what Her The Hobbit & Lost Characters Have in Common.* [online] Available at: <http://www.accesshollywood.com/articles/evangeline-lilly-on-what-her-the-hobbit-lost-characters-have-in-common-140891> [Accessed 21 November 2016].

Miller, C., 2016. *Analysis of The Force Awakens – Rey: A Hero's Awakening.* [online] Available at: <http://www.starwarsreport.com/2016/02/03/analysis-of-the-force-awakens-rey-a-heros-awakening> [Accessed 18 November 2016].

Pulver, A., 2015. *Star Wars Director J. J. Abrams: We Always Wanted Women at the Center of The Force Awakens.* [online] Available at: <http://www.rawstory.com/2015/12/star-wars-director-jj-abrams-we-always-wanted-women-at-the-center-of-the-force-awakens> [Accessed 12 January 2017].

Rottenberg, J., 2013. *The Hobbit': Evangeline Lilly as Tauriel.* [online] Available at: < http://ew.com/article/2013/06/05/evangeline-lilly-hobbit-desolation-of-smaug/?utm_source=feedburner&utm_medium=feed&utm_campaign=Feed%253A+entertainmentweekly%252Flatest+(Entertainment+Weekly%253A++Today%2527s+Latest)&utm_content=Google+Reader)> [Accessed 18 November 2016].

Rucka, G., 2015. *Star Wars Before the Awakening.* Glendale, CA: Disney-Lucasfilm Press.

Scaefer, E., 2016. *Star Wars The Force Awakens: Rey's Story*. Glendale, CA: Disney-Lucasfilm Press.

Shaw-Williams, H., 2013. *Hobbit: Desolation of Smaug Evangeline Lilly's Tauriel Is Young and Ruthless*. [online] Available at: <http://screenrant.com/hobbit-deoslation-smaug-evangeline-lilly-tauriel-interview> [Accessed 17 January 2017].

Star Wars: The Force Awakens. 2015. [DVD] Directed by J.J. Abrams. USA: Walt Disney Studios Motion Pictures.

Stock, L., 2017. *Rey to the Rescue!* London: Dorling Kindersley.

Szostak, P., 2015. *The Art of Star Wars: The Force Awakens*. New York: Abrams Books.

The Hobbit: The Desolation of Smaug. 2013. [DVD] Directed by Peter Jackson. New Zealand/USA: New Line Cinema.

The Hobbit: The Battle of the Five Armies. 2014. [DVD] Directed by Peter Jackson. New Zealand/USA: New Line Cinema.

Tolkien, J. R. R., 1937. *The Hobbit, or There and Back Again*. Reprint 1965. Translated from English by I. Horea, 2013. Bucharest: Rao.

Tolkien, J. R. R., 1999 (1977). *The Silmarillion*. C. Tolkien ed. London: HarperCollinsPublishers.

Tolkien, J.R.R., 1980. *Unfinished Tales of Númenor and Middle-earth*. C. Tolkien ed. Translated from English by I. Horea, 2011. Bucharest: Rao.

Tracey, J., 2015. *The Doom Star. Jedi Killers, and Other Early Changes to Star Wars: The Force Awakens*. [online] Available at: <https://www.outerplaces.com/science-fiction/item/10776-the-doom-star-jedi-killers-and-other-early-changes-to-star-wars-the-force-awakens> [Accessed 8 October 2016].

Ward, J., 2015. *Rey from Star Wars The Force Awakens Aint'a Mary Sue*. [online] Available at: <http://makingstarwars.net/2015/12/rey-from-star-wars-the-force-awakens-aint-a-mary-sue> [Accessed 8 October 2016].

Weintraub, S., 2013. *Evangeline Lilly Talks the Origin of Her Character*. [online] Available at: <http://collider.com/evangeline-lilly-hobbit-the-desolation-of-smaug-interview> [Accessed 14 January 2017].

Biographies
(for more information visit www.lunapresspublishing.com)

Hazel Butler (UK) MA Celtic Archaeology, Academic Researcher (Gender identity and Iron Age archaeology). Fantasy Author and Copywriter.

A J Dalton (UK), PhD Creative Writing. Fantasy author with Gollancz.

Alina Hadîmbu (Romania), MA in Comparative Literature and Cultural Anthropology. Writer.

Jyrki Korpua (Finland), PHD in Literary studies and Lecturer. Researcher.

Rostislav Kůrka (Czech Republic/Finland) MA Theology. Researcher, Writer.

Kim Lakin-Smith (UK) MA in Journalism and Creative Writing, Fantasy and Science Fiction writer.

Juliet McKenna (UK) Greek and Roman history and literature. Fantasy Writer.

Anna Milon (Russia), English Literature, current Education Officer of the Tolkien Society. Researcher.

Cheryl Morgan (UK) SF critic and publisher, owner of Wizard's Tower Press and Hugo Award winner. Researcher.

Lorianne Reuser (Canada) English Literature, Greek and Roman studies. Researcher.

www.ingramcontent.com/pod-product-compliance
Lightning Source LLC
Chambersburg PA
CBHW071339080526
44587CB00017B/2890